The Function of Dance
in Human Society

THE FUNCTION OF

DANCE

IN HUMAN SOCIETY

A Seminar Directed by Franziska Boas

DANCE HORIZONS

1801 EAST 26 STREET, BROOKLYN, N.Y. 11229

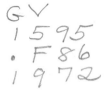

One of a series of republications by Dance Horizons
1801 East 26th Street, Brooklyn, New York 11229

This is an unabridged republication of the first edition
published in 1944 by The Boas School, New York

Standard Book Number 87127-032-3

Library of Congress Catalog Card Number 71-181478

Printed in the United States of America

Preface to the Second Edition

SINCE 1942 when this Seminar was presented, dance has made tremendous headway toward becoming a true part of the life of this country. At that time it was necessary to study "primitive" and "exotic" cultures in order to realize how dance could fulfill a vital role in the life of peoples. For us as members of the "Western Christian Civilization" dance was only one of those frills of entertainment or a downright evil. At last dance in modern society is acquiring the natural function which it had and still has in those less mechanized and less guilt-ridden cultures.

One of the most helpful signs for its growth is the proliferation of activity in many fields for the layman such as dance therapy for the mentally and emotionally ill, for the maladjusted, for the retarded, for the physically handicapped, including spastics; dance for the blind, for the deaf, for the elderly. There is more dance in education—pre-school, elementary, secondary and college. Dance notation has advanced and been accepted as a reading and writing tool both for dancers and for workers in other fields of movement. Dance has contributed to the understanding and development of non-verbal research being carried out in "kinesics." There are groups to encourage research and writing about dance.

Dance in the theatre, concerts, films and television offers a great variety of types and styles. One very interesting development is that dancers are performing for the people in the street and in the parks. (In the thirties when the New Dance Group was organized they tried to bring dance to the people, but "the people" were not yet ready for them.) Now people are asking for the opportunity to participate. We may be experiencing a revival similar to the wandering bards, mimes and jongleurs of the Middle Ages. There is even dance in religion again. Part of this movement is toward so-called environmental dance: environments either already present in natural form or constructed before or during the dance action. One may come upon performances in progress while wandering through the streets and parks of some of our cities.

These developments did not just happen. Over the years dancers discovered that technique alone could not bring about a vital art. Part of the stimulus came as an acceptance and participation in what Mary Wigman and Hanya Holm had been advocating for years, namely the use of the medium of improvisation to free creative action and to control form. There has also been a far greater involvement in non-European cultures and philosophies. All of this has brought about many changes in dance and its application to other fields.

A very important stimulant to the growth of dance has been the funding of individual dancers and dance companies to a much greater extent than in the past, by national, state and private organizations and individuals. Interviews with dancers and dance teachers on radio and television and special performances choreographed for television bring dance into more remote sections of the country. Dance, which was formerly confined to large cities, is now a part of smaller communities.

Men and women, both young and old, have discovered that participation in dance activity is not limited to the professional dancer but that they may find a renewal of life, a stimulus of creative action and certainly a better understanding of the intricacies of human nature, through actual doing. This participation by the man in the street leads to interest in the activity of the artist. The more dance becomes a part of community life, the greater will be the role of the dance artist and his performing group in supplying stimulus and pleasure to the life of all.

This sounds Utopian to those who struggled with dance in the twenties and thirties and even in the forties. Even though there is recognition of the great value of dance to society, the need for more professional paying positions in all of the above mentioned areas still exists.

This short overview indicates that there is much for dance to accomplish and that there are many fields of work for dancers of imagination and courage. May they become involved in the life of the country and the world.

I wish to thank the speakers for permission to republish their papers and photographs: Geoffrey Gorer for revisions and the use of illustrations from his book "Africa Dances" (reprinted by W. W. Norton & Co., Inc in the Norton Library 1962), also Norton for help in securing these illustrations; the Indonesian Consulate General in New York and Margaret Mead for securing new illustrations for the article "Form and Function of Dance in Bali," (This article was included in "Traditional Balinese Culture" edited by Jane Belo, Columbia University Press 1970.) and Paulina Buhl for her editorial help.

Franziska Boas

Rome, Georgia
June 1971

Contents and Contributors

Illustrations

□□

KWAKIUTL INDIANS: Mother rocking cradle

KWAKIUTL INDIANS: Raven mask of cannibal-dancer

KWAKIUTL INDIANS: Salmon-dancer

KWAKIUTL INDIANS: Chief with copper money-sheet

KWAKIUTL INDIANS: The return of the Hamatsa

AFRICA: Dapango war dance

AFRICA: The dancers of Danané

AFRICA: Totem dancers at Javara, I – Antelope

AFRICA: The Dead Cannibal, I—Mask dancing

AFRICA: The Dead Cannibal, I—Masks enter the village at dawn

AFRICA: The Dead Cannibal, II – Dancing after funeral

HAITI: Congo Société at Mardi Gras

HAITI: Congo Société at Mardi Gras

HAITI: Congo Société at Mardi Gras

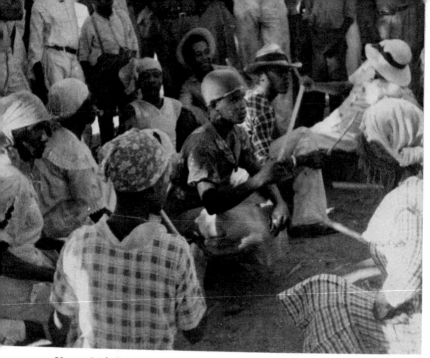

HAITI: Stick-dancers, all men

HAITI: Danse Gabienne

BALI: Bird of Ill Omen, in Legong

BALI: Djanger dancer, "a feeling of relaxation and detachment"

BALI: Masked figures of servants, dressed and posing to exhibit masks for photography. Sanoer, from mask collection of Pidanda Made

BALI: Mario takes a pupil by the wrists and swings him across the dancing space, in Tabanan

BALI: (1) Male dancer impersonating female, theatricals accompany Barong from Tatag; (2) Girl impersonating prince figure, Ardja theatrical with Barong from Pakadowi; (3) Baris for ceremony of Saba Jeh in Peloedoe; (4) Dancer accompanying Barong from Tiga, servant (tjondong). All photos taken at Bajoeng Gede.

Introductory Note

THIS seminar on the Function of Dance in Human Society was presented simply as an introductory investigation of the relationship between dance and the way of life. Primitive and exotic cultures were turned to, because in them the dance has a really vital function, and its meaning is accepted by the community. Only a homogeneous community can develop an art which is understood by all. In our Western culture, the varieties of nationalities, of interests, and of opportunities prevent the development of any large homogeneous group. Instead, we have many small, separate groups, composed of differing peoples, with varying philosophies. Only a variety of expression in life and in art can fulfill the needs of these peoples.

In dance there are decorative, impressionistic, and expressionistic forms, just as in the other arts. The styles and forms of any art are dictated by the concept of beauty which has been built up in a given community. Symbolism may be read into these forms, or new forms may be developed through direct symbolic representation. But the final form of the dance which the community supports will be affected by the styles accepted in that community. The more personal the symbols, the less broadly understandable the dance will be, and the less acceptance and support it can logically expect.

Dance today is primarily expressionistic. The only dance form which has a style and a symbolism that can appeal to a large group is the ballet. This style of dance has existed in some form or other over a very extensive period of time, and in practically all the countries of the European-American hemisphere, as also in those countries within the Western sphere of influence. This may account for the up-swing of interest in ballet forms at the present time, since people from the northern, southern, and eastern parts of the world are coming to us, and are interesting themselves in our dance. However, since more and more of our people are, at the same time, coming into contact with other cultures, and are finding new ways of living, and are exploring new ideas and movements, the ballet has lost its meaning for many groups and individuals.

I question, therefore, the wisdom of modern dancers in turning back to the ballet-form when they find themselves without a large following for the newer, less stylized forms. These dancers are giving up in midstream. Instead of widening their communities of support by attracting more of the people whose new experiences and interests might help them to understand new symbols in movement, they are turning back to mere artifices of movement, instead of progressing toward true meaning and expression. Thus they are trying to prolong the life of a style in dance whose symbolisms are drawn from and directed to only one of the groups in our culture.

Modern dance must continue to explore the ways of men and women in all their activities. It must learn from the movements and philosophies of all age groups and all types; from the healthy and from the physically handicapped, from the mentally integrated and from the neurotic. It must learn from the successful action and interaction of small and large groups; from war and from peace. It must turn into its own substance the experience of working people in every sort of occupation and industry, going to and from work, and during their work and at play.

Modern dance in America must absorb characteristic material from the many peoples that have come here, and must make fluid their individuality to the degree where their native heritage of motion, of outlook, and of expression is available in implementing our dance.

We must start again, humbly, at the bottom of the ladder. We must be willing to study and judge and—if necessary—destroy our own gods, particularly those of style, if we are to find contact with the life of the people of today. Dance must be thought of as an expression of communal activity, and its constructive social influence on the individual must be realized and promoted. The possibilities of dance as mental therapy must be explored just as, until now, its uses in physical training have been emphasized. The psychological implications of dance, and the methods of using it as a broadening educative medium on a par with the other arts must be widely understood and propagandized.

The material of this symposium is published in the hope that it may stimulate thought and better understanding of the wealth of sources there are to drawn on, within and outside of the framework of our culture. It is hoped also that other groups will be interested to the point of carrying on similar projects. For their part in helping in the instigation of just such interest as this publication represents, I wish to thank the speakers for permission to publish their papers and photographs, Claire Holt and Romana Javitz for their help in organizing the entire project, Clark Wissler and the Harmon Foundation for their generosity in making available material for the exhibits displayed during the seminar, and, for relieving much of the tedium and detail of editing, Jan Gay and G. Legman.

Franziska Boas

Spring 1944

Dance and Music in the Life of the
Northwest Coast Indians of North America

By Franz Boas

I N DISCUSSING the social function of the dance among the Kwakiutl Indians of Vancouver Island, British Columbia, I shall make only occasional remarks in regard to the technique and form of their dances. Practically every aspect of Kwakiutl life is accompanied by some form of dance, from the cradle to the grave.

When the infant lies in its cradle, which is suspended from an elastic branch, the mother has the end of the branch connected by a rope to her toes, and by moving her foot rhythmically, the cradle is made to swing up and down, while at the same time the mother sings a lullaby. When the child is a little older and able to sit and stand, the father will dance it on his knee, and sing a cradle song at the same time. He will sing thus to his little son:

"When I am a man I shall be a hunter, O father, ya ha ha ha
When I am a man I shall be a harpooner, O father, ya ha ha ha
When I am a man I shall be a canoe-builder, O father, ya ha ha ha
When I am a man I shall be a board-maker, O father, ya ha ha ha
When I am a man I shall be a workman, O father, ya ha ha ha
That there may be nothing of which you shall be in want, O father, ya ha ha ha."

Or to a little girl:

"Our treasure came here to dig clams for her mother and her old slave, ahe ahe ya
Our treasure came here to get clover for her mother and her old slave, ahe ahe ya
O mother, make me a basket that I may pick salmon berries and salal berries and huckleberries for my old slave, ahe ahe ya
Let him get ready who is to be my husband that he may be ready to help my mother and my old slave, ahe ahe ya."

When the children get older they have play songs and dances. For instance they will play "pretending to be asleep." They sit down in a circle and then lie down. Suddenly the leader shouts: "Now we'll be awake!" They all jump up and form a line following the leader who leads them dancing in circles and intricate movements, crawling under the arms of various couples in a way similar to that of our children. Then, accompanied by the sound of a drum, they will dance in a circle, performing various antics. In olden times they used to have the whole body whitened for the last of these performances.

When they are still older, the young men will be seen marching and dancing along the streets singing love-songs which are intended to embarrass the girls:

"You are hard-hearted, you are hard-hearted, my dear, ha ha ye ya ha ha

You are cruel, you are cruel, my dear, ha ha ye ya ha ha

I am tired of waiting for you, I am tired of waiting for you, my dear, ha ha ye ya ha ha

Now I shall cry all on account of my dear, ha ha ye ya ha ha

Ha, I shall go down to the lower world and I shall cry for you, my dear, ha ha ye ya ha ha."

At other times they sing gambling songs. The gamblers sit in two long rows opposite each other. Their gambling songs are accompanied by drum beating, and they move their bodies rhythmically according to the rhythms of the song. The object of the game is to guess who is holding a gambling stick which is being hidden in their hands. During the dance movements they move their arms rapidly, crossing each other's, and thus pass the stick back and forth, while the other party has to guess where it is. Generally there are no words accompanying these songs, but merely syllables like "ya he ya ha." The dance movements of the upper body are extremely lively.

The most elaborate and important dances are those performed during Kwakiutl social and religious ceremonies. On the whole these are all solo dances. In the social dances the dancer appears frequently, his face covered by a mask which represents the ancestor of the family. The movements of the dance are all performed essentially in the knees. The Indians themselves, in evaluating the perfection of the dance, always speak of the ability of the dancer to use his or her knees well. In most of the social dances, the dancer raises his hands, the fingers trembling with very great rapidity, the body moving at the same time from right to left and from left to right. When the dancing songs describe any particular actions, these will be indicated pantomimically by the dancer whenever the significant words occur in the text of the song.

Group dances are very rare. They occur for instance in the Wolf dance, in which a large number of men appear wearing headmasks of the wolf on their foreheads, leaving their faces free. They move in a circle around the fire in the middle of the house, stooping, holding their hands with fingers folded, the thumbs up.

In every solo dance the performer is accompanied by an assistant who carries a staff in the right hand, a rattle in the left. In the religious dances it is customary for the women who sit in the audience to rise every now and then from their seats and to dance standing, in order to please the performer.

The sacred dances are extremely varied in character and in purpose. The most important ceremony is that of the Cannibal dancer, who is supposed to bite pieces of flesh from the arms of the bystanders and who, it is said, in olden times would kill slaves and partake of their flesh. Whenever he appears, the spectators who are sitting around the walls of the square house watch the ceremony in fear and trembling.

When the Cannibal dancer first appears, he jumps down from the roof of the house. His face is blackened. He wears rings of cedar bark on his head and around his neck, and is covered with eagle down. He dances in a crouching position around the fire, his steps slow and almost crawling. After a while he disappears into a sacred room set aside for this purpose. When he comes out again he dances in a standing position with high, slow steps. Generally the rhythm of this song is in five parts, and the movements correspond. The following is an example of one of the songs sung for him:

"I went all around the world trying to get food, all around the world

I went all around the world trying to get human beings, trying to get human beings, all around the world

I went all around the world trying to get skulls, trying to get skulls, all around the world

I went all around the world trying to get corpses, trying to get corpses, all around the world

Food is always being put into my mouth, food is always being put into my mouth, therefore I am supernatural

I am always swallowing life, I am always swallowing life, my food is alive

Property is always being put into my mouth, property is always being put into my mouth, property is my food."

When singing the fifth verse, the dancer will move his hands, indicating how the food is being put into his mouth. In the same way the swallowing is indicated by a movement of the hands down in front of the body. The Cannibal dancer is always accompanied by several assistants who hold him by his neck ring when he tries to attack any of the bystanders.

One of the most complicated dances is the so-called war dance which is always performed by a woman. The dancer wears rings of hemlock branches and enters the room with very short steps, resting long on one foot and then making a short step forward with the other foot. She holds her arms with the elbows close to the body, the forearms stretched forward with palms upward. This movement indicates that she is trying to conjure up supernatural power from underground.

According to the general rules of movement in these ceremonials, she enters the house, turns completely around to the left, and then proceeds to the right around the fire with her short steps. When she reaches the middle of the rear of the house she turns again, and then proceeds until she reaches the door. Then she turns still again, and the circuit of the fire is repeated four times. When she reaches the rear of the house the fourth time, she moves rapidly backward and forward with short steps, looks down to the ground, and suddenly closes her hands. She is supposed to have caught the supernatural power in her hands. This power she then throws with a wide swinging movement against the audience, who falls down at once trying to escape it, for if the power entered the body it might cause disease.

In other cases she may apparently bring out of the ground a frog or a snake that is made to move about by invisible strings. This dance is always accompanied by some kind of trickery. For instance she may ask one of the bystanders to spear her. The selected person will take a spear and put it in her side, and at once blood streams out. Apparently he pushes it into her body until it comes out at the opposite side, where blood is also seen to flow down. Then the medicine man is called to cure her, and by stroking his hand over her body, he causes the stream of blood to stop and apparently cures her. This trick is effected by attaching bladders filled with blood on both sides of her chest, the one on the side opposite the spear-thrust being provided with a hook attached to her upper arm, by means of which hook she can tear the bladder at the proper moment.

Still another dance represents the story of a boy who acquired supernatural power when scaling a mountain. He was given the ability to fly, and the dance represents how he arrives at his home. A long board is placed in the house slanting up to the roof with a small platform at the upper end. The dancer appears on the platform, dressed completely in hemlock branches. Then he runs down the slanting board with very short steps and dances on the floor of the house. Sinuous motions of the whole body indicate the movements of a bird. He dances around the fire and then with short rapid steps and constant movements of the body he runs up the plank, turns at the top and comes down again. This is repeated four times.

When these dances are finished there is a long ceremony of purification of the dancers. Prescribed motions are important in this ceremony also. The most characteristic one is the purification of the body of the dancer by having him pass through a large ring of cedar bark in a prescribed way. First he has to put his right arm up through the ring which is then gradually lowered, rubbing his body all over, and when finally the ring reaches the floor, the dancer must step out with the right foot first, turn around completely, to take the left foot out of the ring, and then, in a ceremonial way, sit down to be washed.

It is impossible to give anything like a complete description of these complicated dances in a short space. They are performed in winter during the months from November to February, and the social life of the tribe during this period centers entirely around the performance of dances of this kind.

During these festivals there are also theatrical performances involving dancing. There is for instance a society of young men called Killer Whales. During the lighter moments of the ceremonial, these young men will come in all dressed as Killer Whales, wearing on their backs dorsal fins made of wood. They make a circuit around the fire, acting like whales, pretending to dive into the water and come up again spouting. This is a purely pantomimic performance, but in other cases there will be more complicated theatricals. Thus the young girls who form a society by themselves during the winter ceremonial will enter the house and say that they want to marry. Then a theatrical performance is arranged following the rules of the marriage ceremony, which also includes formal dances.

Dances are also performed on the return of a war party. When the canoes approach the home village after a successful raid, the warriors stand up in their canoes dancing and singing, holding in their hands the heads of the slain enemies. When they reach the beach of the village they are met by the women and others who stayed at home, all of whom come down dancing. With great ceremony and more dances the heads are put up on a scaffolding erected in front of the houses, as the symbol of victory.

Finally, when death comes to an important man a mourning ceremony is held. First of all, his wife or mother goes down to the beach, scratches her cheeks until they bleed, and then, sitting down, recites the whole family history from the very beginning when the first ancestor came down from heaven in the form of a bird and assumed the shape of a man. Meanwhile the men assemble in a house and, beating the rhythm with stones, they recite in songs the deeds of the deceased, accompanying the song with appropriate movements.

It will be seen from the foregoing that song and dance accompany all the events of Kwakiutl life, and that they are an essential part in the culture of the people. Song and dance are inseparable here. Although there are expert performers, everyone is obliged to take part in the singing and dancing, so that the separation between performer and audience that we find in our modern society does not occur in more primitive society such as that represented by the Kwakiutl Indians.

Discussion:

(FRANZISKA BOAS:) The Kwakiutl Indians are one of many tribes living along the North-Pacific coast of North America. They are essentially fisher folk living on the east coast of Vancouver Island and the shore of the mainland opposite. The villages are scattered along the coast, and each one consists of a single row of houses facing the sea and fronting a level street which is built high enough to be out of reach of the highest tides. Steps lead down to the beach where the canoes are tied up. The houses are large square buildings with unobstructed space in the center. A raised platform about five feet wide runs along the walls. Several families live in one house, and each has a bedroom built on the platform. The roof is covered with loose boards that can be moved aside to allow the smoke of the fires to escape.

During the summer the people scatter to fish for their winter supply of food. In the winter they come back to the villages to live in their permanent houses. Here they lead a very social life. Often groups of men wander through the streets from house to house, singing. They sing love songs or songs about people who have gone away or songs describing things that have happened to people. In the winter-time groups of families come together for the evening meal in one of the houses, and these meals are always accompanied by feast songs. There is always a song-leader who calls out the words. In summer the rhythm is given by hand-clapping; in winter—the time of ceremonials—with baton and drums.

One of the important institutions of these Indians is the potlatch, a distribution of property between families which serves the purpose of establishing the social standing of the person who distributes the goods. The receiver is obligated to return at another potlatch at least as much as he has received. The custom is comparable to that existing among members of our society of competition in debutante coming-out parties, dinner parties, card parties, costume balls, the giving of wedding gifts, etc. Among the Kwakiutl, as in our society, this is in part economically determined. The Kwakiutl can supply themselves with more food and material than each family needs. They can therefore give away, use, and waste as much as they wish. They can give away everything and know they will get it back at another potlatch.

The potlatch is also a means of validating any action, because of the inability of the Kwakiutl to write their own language. All transactions must therefore be made in public, and no person can attain to any position without a public ceremony intended to apprise both him and the group of his new privileges and responsibilities. The Kwakiutl love speeches, and these are always very elaborate. The person who is giving the feast or distributing property usually has a speaker who makes his speech for him. He may then say a few words himself. The speaker always carries a staff in his hand with which he emphasizes his words by pressing the end into the ground and bending his knees. The typical potlatch speech shows clearly the exaggerated feeling of greatness held so much in esteem among the Kwakiutl.

There are also religious ceremonials and feasts. The dances to be described belong to these ceremonials. Every participant in the ceremonial is supposed to be initiated in solitude by a supernatural Being. After his initiation he returns from the woods and his dance is, in part, a pantomimic performance in which the powers of the spirit that initiated him are symbolized. These spirits are abroad only during the winter, and for this reason the ceremony and the dances connected with it are performed only during that season and are commonly called the Winter Ceremonial. During the ceremony, the family-fires within the house are removed, a large single fire is built in the center of the house, and a sacred room is erected in the rear. Whole tribes visit one another to participate in these ceremonials, and the guests sit in the rear of the house, the front being reserved for the uninitiated.

Although the novices are supposed to be initiated by encounters with supernatural beings, not everyone is free to meet them. The right to be initiated is rather a prerogative transmitted from a father to his son, daughter, or son-in-law. It is he who sends out the youth to be initiated, who awaits his return, and at the proper time invites the ecstasy of the youth. More than that, he asks for their assistance in bringing back the novice, who shuns the odor of secular human beings. The novice must be captured by appropriate ceremonies, led back, and restored to a secular status. The patron of the novice is thus responsible for a great feast which lasts many days and which is part and parcel of the lavish distribution of food and property in the potlatch. He is paying for the services of those who help him in his efforts to capture the novice and calm his holy frenzy. The novice then receives a sacred name, which indicates his membership among the initiates of the Winter Ceremonial, and the renown of the patron is redoubled by the lavishness of his expenditures.

The capture of the novice is brought about by various dances that are supposed to attract him. These are performed by former initiates who execute each his own dance. According to tradition many of these are the dances belonging to ancestors who lived at an early time when men were still animals. There is no inner connection between the various dances, but the leaders of the ceremonial who hold hereditary office select the performers and determine the order of the dances beforehand.

The Kwakiutl make use of many occasions to make speeches and sing songs, also to pay off their debts contracted during the potlatch ceremonies. The occasion of the religious ceremonies is also made use of for this purpose. Before the novice returns and the real ceremony begins, there are numerous dances by other persons who are inheriting positions from their fathers or mothers. There is a great deal of show of wealth and standing in speeches, songs, and potlatches, as with mock contempt for wealth by breaking a piece from one of the large, roughly rectangular copper plates which pass as money of high denomination among the Kwakiutl; or by reference for instance to Dzonoqua, a monster with hollow eyes and open mouth, shouting "O-o-o-o" and eating children.

The real ceremony opens in the evening after a secret meeting in the woods. Four inviters go, one after another, to each house in the village in turn, entering and telling the people to come to the assembly house for the Winter Ceremonial. This is repeated four times. After the third call the guests assemble. Then the inviters go once more to call whoever may have stayed away. The people are seated, and amuse themselves while eating their supper, which is served by the young men of the host's family. The dishes are cleared away, and suddenly the leader of the ceremonial enters the door swinging a rattle. The supernatural power has entered the house and everyone is quiet. No laughter, no conversation is permitted. It is essential from this point on that neither the novice nor any one of the singers and attendants make a mistake in movement, rhythm, or song, for this excites not only the novice but also all the old initiates, and results in a general state of frenzy. Singers beat time and sing simultaneously. Some of the dancers sing while they dance, and follow the changing time-beat of the song. The song-leader must beat time for the songs with a long bottle-shaped baton, and all the singers watch him and keep time with his beat. If any of them makes a mistake and beats time too fast or too slowly, the Fool dancers and Grizzly Bear dancers, who police the ceremonial, become excited. Immediately the singers stop singing, and beat fast time.

In one instance the man who made the mistake in his time-beating arose and said: "What can I say to you, Sparrows? [The managers of the ceremonial] It is not your fault that I made a mistake in my time-beating. Now I will promise a feast, Shamans, and I give fifty blankets for this." Then the master of ceremonies spoke and said: "This is the reason why our grandfathers were always very careful with their batons. You see how much it has cost our friend. This is not my wish. It is handed down to us from our ancestors, to whom it was given by the Winter Ceremonial maker."

Since it is so important to make no mistakes in the time-beating, not all singers are allowed to beat time when a good dancer performs to a song with complicated rhythm. In former years the Fool dancers and the Grizzly Bears are said to have killed a dancer who made a mistake. Nowadays the punishment is merely performed symbolically, for the Fool dancers carry lances with tips that slide into the handle, with which they pretend to kill the offender.

After the leader of the ceremonial has entered, the singers strike up a song, and a dancer, perhaps the Thunderbird dancer, enters. He turns around counterclockwise as he enters, and dances around the central fire, also counterclockwise; turns again in the rear of the house, and proceeds. Thus he circles around the fire four times. A new song is struck up, and a new dancer, perhaps the Wasp, appears. He moves around the fire in the same direction as the preceding dancer, but with his own characteristic movements. After each dance, the master of ceremonies listens for the song and whistles of the returning novice. Finally the climax is reached. Attracted by the dances, the new initiate approaches. His song is heard louder and louder. Whistles—the voices of the supernatural powers—shriek, and he bursts into the house through the door or by jumping down from the loosely slatted roof. With this the formal dance of the new initiate begin.

Most dances consist of four divisions corresponding to four stanzas of the song. A composer makes up the tune, and after he has composed it he gives it to the man who wants to use it, and asks him for the words to be sung. The song then belongs to the man who has the words, that is, to the dancer. After each stanza the dancer disappears into the sacred room from which he then emerges with new decorations. The first dance was generally performed naked, with a neck-ring, head-ring, girdle, wristlets, and anklets of hemlock branches. Nowadays, because of the pressure of civilized prudery, the dancers are clothed in Western attire, at least from the waist down, beneath their own artistic decorations. In the second dance, the body of the dancer is usually completely covered, and he wears a mask. This is not really a dance but an exhibition parade of the mask and is performed by a helper. The third circuit finds the dancer dressed in blankets and cedar-bark neck- and head-rings, while in the fourth he again wears a mask.

Practically all of these dances are solos, in contrast to the usual group dances of the Pueblos of New Mexico. Every dancer is accompanied by a man, an attendant who carries a rattle or a staff. This attendant does not dance, but merely walks or stands next to the dancer. The Cannibal dancer has four attendants who hold him by the neck-ring when he becomes too menacing. Both men and women perform important dances, most of them having the same titles but varying according to the traditional movements attributed to men and women. There are certain dances performed only by men, such as the Cannibal dance, although women perform a similar dance called the Eater. The War dance is performed only by women.

Most of the dances begin in the rear of the house behind the fire, facing the drummers and song-leader. The main part of the dance is performed in the space between the fire and the singers and drummers. All dances have fixed gestures and rhythms. In the Cannibal dance, the woman's War dance, and some others, there is a fixed fundamental gesture like a basso ostinato that is broken at intervals by special gestures of pantomimic character which are descriptive of the text of the song. Since songs belong to particular individuals, there are always slight variations in the phrasing of rhythm and gesture depending on the family of the performer and on the words of the song. This is due to the belief that "the spirits appeared to the ancestors of the various clans of different tribes, but gave each of his proteges his powers in a slightly different form."

The rhythm of the vocal dance accompaniment, as well as of the beating, is exceedingly complex; but the most distinguishing characteristic is the fact that the beating as well as the dance movement which is associated with it, is often syncopated. In the beating it is caused by the arm being raised when the tone is uttered and by falling immediately afterwards. In the dancing, it is caused by a distinctly separated stretch and bend of the knee over each step no matter how fast or slow the sequence of steps. The characteristic dance posture is with the body bent slightly forward from the hips. The steps are generally small, with the feet very close to the ground and almost always on the whole foot. The weight is transferred to the leg as the knee straightens. The knee is then bent as the other leg lifts. This gives an accent down. When the accent in the movement is up, the weight is transferred with the knee bent, and the knee straightens as the other leg lifts. In some cases, such as the fourth Cannibal dance, the legs are lifted very high, but the knee action is still present. In fact the most outstanding element in their dance technique is this knee action.

The arm movements vary for men and women with regard to freedom of sweep. A good female dancer uses only the lower arm. The elbows are kept well against the sides of the body. The hand is loosely stretched, the fingers together. The typical woman's dance gesture is with one hand at the side, up at shoulder level, and the other in front, down at waist height. The lower arms are swung from one side to the other, the head taking the opposite direction. The palm of the lower hand is forward. This gesture may be used in any woman's dance at any time. It is also used by the male dancer as filler between other gestures. The male dancer, however, is also allowed to use his entire arm. The hand takes on the same form as the woman's. A good dancer may take liberties with the movement, and increase its sweep and its position in relation to the rest of the body. Rhythm variations may be made in the legs only.

Another characteristic dance movement is the quivering of the hands

15

as well as of the entire body. The vibration in the hands is produced by a very rapid bending and stretching of the straight fingers at their base, where they join the metacarpals. The thumb is held quiet. The man may also vibrate the whole hand from the wrists. The body vibration is peculiar to the Shaman. There is also a vibration of the lower jaw. The body vibration can be produced only when the body becomes almost fixed in certain positions producing strong counter-tension to the desired gesture. All of these vibrations require a definite ecstatic quality in order to be executed. When inquiring of an Indian how it is done technically, he can only say: "When my excitement reaches a certain point, and my knee is bent so, then I begin to vibrate." Only the best dancers can vibrate with the entire body and the jaw. The vibration of the fingers is never used in the War or Ghost dance.

It is important to note that we find here a very highly stylized art with a rhythmic and dance vocabulary corresponding to the speeds, types of rhythms, types of steps, and movements. We have no complete list of these names as yet, but the clarity of the various ideas in the mind of the Indian is such as to allow of nearly ten named rhythms and a similar number of steps. The gestures, too, are named, for instance the trembling or vibration of the hands is called Xwuléquóla or Hroléquóla.

This culture is full of drama and magic and is, as we have seen, closely bound up with the life of the people. We find here community participation with emphasis on the individual achievement. It would be interesting to ask whether such a close relation between dance and the people is found in all primitive cultures . . .

Q:

Does the dance express the life of people as a whole in all cultures? Dance expresses such different people so often. Consider the Pueblo of the Southwest; it is hard to say whether these are more closely knit than those of the Plains. But the cultural characteristic of the Pueblo is formality with emphasis on repetition. Drawing something out of the earth is representative. This Pueblo emphasis is so different from that of the Kwakiutl, who gathers supernatural power from the atmosphere and throws it in the air . . . Was any mis-step penalized among the Kwakiutl? . . .

(FRANZ BOAS:) The forms are very strict, particularly in their rhythm. Not only mis-steps, but errors in beating time were severly punished. In a great many cases there were pretended errors too. I remember the following case quite long ago, fifty years ago, when I was there first. A certain man wanted an excuse to give a potlatch. He had a dancer make a mis-step in order to be punished to give a potlatch. But there are much more serious cases. They had one of these performances like the Sun dance of the Plains Indians. The dancer had his muscles perforated and was hung up by them. A certain kind of dancer danced or stood under him with a lance. If the cords broke he fell on the lance. I have not seen that myself, but I know they did it. It is curious to get a psychological insight on these people. On the one hand, the dance is very sacred, on the other it affords an opportunity for fun, demonstrations, and horse-play. You might say it is a constant change of attitude from sacred to entertainment. There are quite a number of illustrative stories, some of which I know are true. For instance, a child came into a room where the father was in some kind of a mask for a performance. Because the child saw him, the father killed the child. There is a peculiar mystic seriousness on the one hand, and entertainment feeling on the other . . .

Q:
In the movement by which the dancer brings up the supernatural power, was the reaction of the people who watched an emotional experience, or were they just going through the motions?

(FRANZ BOAS:) Those particular ones went through the motions, but when the dance is really performed in winter, there is terrible, incredible excitement. In one performance of this kind the women got so frightened they broke down the sides of the house and ran out. But it is very difficult to judge what is real and what is unreal. Certain people sometimes think there is something behind it, but sometimes it is pure fraud . . .

Q:
Where is the center of weight and gravity located in these dances in contrast to the Balinese? . . . We must begin to distinguish between the body awareness of each group—Balinese, Indians, or whatever we see. It is in each case altogether different. There is a different feeling, a different concept of rhythm, of movement, of tension; and the concentration is in different places in these Indian dances than in the Balinese . . .

What is the relation of ordinary movement in everyday activity to the movements of the dance? . . . This involves the relation between motor pattern and dance.

(FRANZ BOAS:) That is probably a very difficult question to answer. The relation between general motor habits and the dance is a complicated matter. I think everyone will agree that when you see an Indian of one tribe walk, you realize it is an entirely different gait from that of another. Although I cannot prove it, I believe that the peculiar dancing movements have to do also with the general habit of walking . . .

Q:

Regarding motor habits; I have noticed in a report by one early explorer that the Kwakiutl in Southern Vancouver Island had a peculiar gait in walking because they used canoes in travelling and were often cramped. The part of the body used in the dance is the part developed in the canoe. There is no articulation of ankles, knees, and shoulders in jump and dance pattern as a whole. Has this been considered? . . .

(FRANZ BOAS:) It might be true. Even among ourselves we find some kind of characteristic gait among seamen on smaller vessels. I do not know if it is an adequate explanation. There are several things to be considered. The whole gesture habit cannot easily be reduced to outer conditions. Some people have free gesture-motions and others have restricted gestures, and these are generally determined by social environment in various ways; but the actual reason is very difficult to determine. We do not know whether we have any kind of detailed investigation which would make clear the sources. We can see how they develop in certain kinds of society. I do not think older people travelled much in canoes and acquired a particular gait in that way. If so, the children would imitate. Imitation in gesture is very strong. It is a most complicated affair . . .

Q:

Women would not be in canoes?
(FRANZ BOAS:) Yes, they would.

Q:

Perhaps some difference in movements would have to do with the general state of relaxation that people have. I know the Navajo behave in a manner contrasting to the Pueblo. Even between movements they relax completely. It gives them a great deal more speed for one thing. It is quite striking, and applies to movements having to do with work, horseback riding, racing, and dancing too. It gives a quite different effect than that given by the Pueblos—an outstanding difference.

Q:

I am impressed with the lightness on the feet, even with difficult bending of the knees . . .

(FRANZ BOAS:) Lightness!

Even in dancing on the plank.

(FRANZ BOAS:) Very complicated . . .

In most Indian dances there is a stamping of the foot which I miss completely among Kwakiutl. Even Blackfeet have the stamp. That is more significant, this lightness, than the cramped position in a canoe.

(FRANZ BOAS:) Don't you think the Pueblo are light?

They stamp, the body goes down with a push. Such a different relation to the earth.

The Function of Different Dance Forms
In Primitive African Communities

By Geoffrey Gorer

I AM appearing here under false pretenses. I know little about West Africa, and even less about dancing. All my experience consists of a four-months' journey which I made through French West Africa nearly eight years ago. I wrote a book about the journey which my publishers insisted on calling "African Dances." Besides this book my only source of knowledge is my undoubtedly very fallible memory, for all my photographs and all the notes which I have not incorporated in my book are somewhere in England.

The people I am going to discuss are some of the cultures inhabiting the enormous stretch of territory called French West Africa. This is a vast piece of land covering the greater part of the bump of the African continent facing the Atlantic Coast with its capital at Dakar. My journey took me on a rough rectangle with Dakar as the top north corner. I traveled east through Senegal and the Sudan and the Ivory Coast, then south through Togoland and Dahomey, west along the Gold Coast and Ivory Coast, and back to Dakar. Over a great deal of this route I looked at dances, for this was one of the main objects of my journey. However, except in two places, I never stopped in one part for more than a few days. The two places in which I stayed longest, Senegal and Dahomey, are the places I am going to discuss. I am also going to say something about the dancing of the various small communities which exist in the dense forest and savannah of the Ivory Coast, for there more than anywhere else is dancing developed and diversified. Except incidentally, I shall not refer to the other regions through which I travelled.

Before I go on to discuss some dances with a certain amount of minuteness, I would like to make a few generalizations about African dancing as a whole. In doing this I am handicapped by a lack of professional vocabulary and professional knowledge; a few movies would be able to make far clearer than I can the various points which seem to me necessary. In their absence, however, I will have to do the best I can with words.

The first and most fundamental point to be made about African dancing is that it always involves the whole body. By this I mean that the typical movement in African dancing are large movements. If the leg is moved, it is moved from the hip rather than from the knee; if the arm is moved, it is moved from the shoulder. All the major muscles of the trunk are involved in most African dances. With very few exceptions there is no subtlety of gesture such as is found among Asian dances, particularly the Javanese, Balinese, Indo-Chinese, or Southern India. The precise control of small movements and small muscles is never the aim of the West African dancer. Another contrast with Asian dancing is that African dancing is dynamic and never, so to speak, static. There is no African dancing where the dancer either stands or sits and moves only a small portion of his body while the rest is stable. African dancing is dynamic with very marked rhythm.

The technique of dancing—the dance steps—are above all acrobatic. In this they have a certain correspondence with the European tradition of classical ballet. By and large, African dancing does not use the same vocabulary as classical ballet, but the virtuosity which can produce such miracles as the fouetté, pirouette, battement, would be thoroughly congenial to the African dance. Some of these acrobatic and semi-acrobatic steps are developed to a pitch of almost incredible virtuosity. They employ a great number of the movements which with us are part of the repertoire of professional acrobats—somersaults, backward jumps, forward saut périlleux, and many other movements which to us would seem isolated, to belong rather to the circus than to the dance.

A further point to make about African dances is that they have very little temporal formality. This phrase is rather obscure, but I cannot immediately think of a better one. The distinction I am trying to make is that between a ballet such as a choreographer designs and contemporary ballroom dancing. Most African dances go on until they stop, whether it be for three minutes or eight days; the formal unit within it, however, is small and is constantly repeated either at the same tempo, or occasionally at a quicker or slower. The best analogy that I can give you for African dancing is the European folksong. This possesses, as you know, a single melody which may last from between thirty seconds to two or three minutes; but, as Constant Lambert once said in writing about some English composers and Ravel's "Bolero—Danse Lascive": "Once you have played a folktune, the only thing you can do is to play it again and play it louder."

I do not wish it to be understood by this that African dancing is monotonous. It generally is not. Most groups of dancers have a relatively large repertoire, and the dancers succeed one another at short intervals and in a fixed order. But a dance with temporal development and formality—that is to say, with a recognizable beginning, middle, and end of fixed proportions—is extreme uncommon. In fact, I saw only two in the more than one hundred African dances I witnessed.

Although African dances employ the time element in the dance so inadequately, they generally make consistent and sophisticated use of the space elements. Practically all African dancing takes place in the open air on special dancing grounds. These are bare and sometimes of very considerable extent. The drummers who give the accompaniment to the dance and who form an integral part of it have nearly always a fixed position, occasionally at the center, but usually at the end furthest from the onlookers. All the African dancing is oriented in relation to the drums; and the use of empty space, of movement through space and of the large composition of the immediately visual element is most carefully and sophisticatedly exploited.

From this statement it will follow that solo dancing is uncommon, and this is a fact. Only in one area—in the forest on the borders of the Ivory Coast and Liberia—are there serious solo dances; and it is in this area that acrobatic virtuosity reaches its highest peak. Elsewhere there may be a little solo dancing in the unimportant spontaneously organized dances for relaxation and diversion, dances without an audience got up because a few young men, or, much more rarely, a few young women, had nothing to do; but the serious dances, the dances which are organized and which are meaningful, always imply a plurality of dancers. The number of people dancing may be anywhere from three to well over a hundred, or even, on a few occasions, the whole population of the village.

The commonest type of dancing is one which employs a group of from eight to sixteen individuals of the same age and sex dancing in unison, nearly always with the most perfect precision and verve. In the more elaborate dances there may be two, three, four or even more groups dancing simultaneously in complementary fashion. These multiple dances only occur in important rituals so charged with varied significance that no one person or group can represent all that is felt to be present at the time.

This brings me to another important point about African dancing. With rare exceptions it is pantomimic and fairly openly so. This is true even of the most acrobatic dances. Again the only exceptions are the unimportant leisure-time dances. This pantomime may be of three sorts. The simplest is direct pantomime—the imitation of a person or animal. This reaches its highest pitch of virtuosity on the Ivory Coast, where animals are mimicked. The dancers wear masks, and costumes made out of animals skins completely covering their bodies. I have seen excellent antelopes, but the most surprising of all were the monkey dances of Odienné. These were two people with sad-looking monkey masks of polished ebony lined with silver, and their bodies were covered with costumes of dark raffia and monkey fur which left their hands and feet bare. They cowered on the ground, searched one another for salt "fleas," scuffled . . . more like monkeys than monkeys usually are. For pure mimicry I have never seen anything like it, but it was barely a dance. It had no form, no beginning or end; they were just monkeys.

The first sort of pantomime, then, is a straightforward imitation of other animals or people. The second form of pantomime is that of the emotion which the dancers hope to feel after they have danced. Typical of this sort of dance is the war dance, in which the movements, the gestures, and the controlled frenzy are all intended to evoke the proper emotions which the warrior will feel when he faces the real enemy.

The third type of pantomime is the representation of abstractions—of the forces of nature; of depersonalized gods. They dance the sea and the river, fertility, and the thunder-storm. This type of dancing is most elaborated in the religious dancing of Dahomey, and I will discuss it at some length later.

In Africa all formal dancing demands special costumes. These are of such tremendous variety in color, material, and form that it is impossible to make any sensible generalizations about them except to say that the dancers nearly always have more of their bodies covered in dancing than in everyday life. Another common practice is for the dancers to wear around their legs, and occasionally around their arms, garters or bracelets so formed that they rattle or jangle at every movement so that the dancer provides his own accompaniment (as do the Spanish dancers with castanets) and with the further effect that when a single dancer in a group moves out of time, not only the visual, but also the auditory harmony is destroyed. Nearly all the costumes too, are essentially decorative and impractical.

One more generalization, and I will have done with them. Outside Senegal there is very little dancing, and that only of a minor character, which does not have extremely important social and—above all—religious functions. There is practically no erotic element in African dancing. It is fairly uncommon for men and women to dance together at the same time; about the only times they do so are in their solemn religious dances. The one exception to this generalization about the absence of erotic dancing is the Cabrai of Northern Togoland. This strange group is one of the anomalies of the area. They wear no clothes at all, and do not share most of the magical religious or social beliefs of their neighbors. Women are in a subordinate position and only men dance; but one of the dances I saw there was both the most obscene and the most surrealist performance I have ever witnessed. With the exception of these few incidences, the dance in West Africa is always an important, and sometimes an overwhelmingly important aspect of the social, esthetic, and religious life of the community.

With this introduction I should like to fix your attention for a little time on the Wolof who live in Senegal in the country near and around Dakar. I have really very little excuse for talking about the Wolof, for they dance less than any group I saw in Africa. I am really talking about them because I like to talk about them; because they have undoubtedly the most elegant, artificial, and dignified civilization that I have ever seen. Even their appearance is more reminiscent of our stereotype of the elegant eighteenth century than of savage Africa. The women wear artificial and highly stylized wigs of sisal; they are elaborately made up with dark blue cosmetics and even tattooing; their manners are as elegantly formalized as those of eighteenth century France. They cultivate assiduously and most successfully all the minor arts of life—elegant and witty conversation, a refined and varied cuisine, tasteful clothes and ornaments, and physical gracefulness.

There are two classes of people in the community who are somewhat our concern. There are the professional musicians and singers, called griots, who are the only people who are allowed to play the available musical instruments—the tom-tom or drums, the balafron, a kind of xylophone, and the kora, a kind of guitar. No music or dancing can take place without these people. The other group which is of some importance is that of the courtesans. These are women who are renowned

25

as much for wit as for complaisance and beauty. Their life is relatively chaste, but they hold salons where the best conversation is heard and the best dancing is seen. The Wolof have all been converted from their native beliefs to either Mohammedanism or Christianity for a great number of generations, and consequently, with one exception, the socially significant dances of the rest of Africa have disappeared from among them.

The dances which take place at the courtesans' houses are social, recreational dances—almost ballroom dances—in which both men and women take part. The most popular of these is the goumbé, which could easily be adapted to Western ballrooms. It is a curious and rather pretty hybrid, having features of both the minuet and the rhumba. This is the pattern of all Wolof social dances.

Although the Wolof have abandoned the greater part of African religion, they retain with the rest of West Africa an enormous fear and dread of sorcerers. A sorcerer is the greatest fear in African life. In some ways the African conception of the sorcerer resembles the Italian conception of people with the evil eye. Sorcerers have the inherited and extremely terrible power of being able to eat other people's souls. Sorcery is inherited through the maternal line, and the child of a sorceress is inevitably a sorcerer himself.

Contrary to the usual belief about primitive magic, the sorcerer's terrible power is only unassailable while the sorcerer is unknown. As soon as he is known and recognized, he can be dealt with either by being killed or by the control of the canonical magicians. The only way that a sorcerer can be recognized is by a clairvoyant in a trance; and it is in the sorcerer-hunting dance—the M'deup dance—that this discovery takes place. The people who are able to recognize a sorcerer in a trance are also called M'deup; they are nearly always women . . . men who fall into a trance and perform the same dance are considered effeminate and debauched.

Miss Holt and Mr. Bateson will tell you about the dancers of Java and Bali who are put into a trance before they start dancing, and then in trance are filled with the supernatural spirits. In Africa the procedure is different: it is the dance itself which is trance-inducing. There are special tom-toms—including one that consists of a bowl inverted in water—which are used for the M'deup dances when there is reason to suppose that a sorcerer is in the neighborhood. As soon as the M'deup hears these drums she starts dancing uncontrollably and most energetically until she falls into the clairvoyant trance. The onlookers dance in the same step from time to time as they feel inclined to keep her company, but the M'deup dances continuously. The M'deup dance is not particularly elegant or varied. It consists of very forcible rhythmic undulating movements of the whole head and torso. The arms are jerked forcibly backwards so that the elbows nearly meet, the knees are slightly bent, and the dancer goes round in circles with small shuffling steps while making these violent physical movements. The M'deup may go on dancing in this way for a very long period before the clairvoyant trance is achieved. Eventually, however, she falls to the ground in a cataleptic fit and stays there for a little time while the drums keep on beating, and the singers sing louder. After a few moments she will go through a curious pantomime, acting as if she had just been awakened from sleep, stretching her arms and staring about. She will open her eyes with her forefingers and touch her ears, nose, and mouth.

After this re-awakening her eyes are almost completely revulsed, so that only the whites are showing, and in this state she will prophesy and name sorcerers. If by any chance there is a sorcerer in the neighborhood, she will fall upon him and scratch and wound him until she is dragged off. When a sorcerer has been pointed out in this fashion, denial is useless, and they will often confess to get the M'deup removed. The M'deup goes into a very profound sleep after she has named the sorcerer, and wakes without any memory of her prophecies.

I have described this dance at length for several reasons. First of all, it is the only type of dance which is found in all communities in West Africa from the most simple to the most complex. Secondly, the technique of using tom-toms and violent motion to induce trance is, as far as I know, unique to this part of the world. Third, this M'deup dance is the only aspect of West African civilization which I have seen as a unit among American Negroes. I have been present at some of the ecstatic services of obscure Negro sects, and in one at least—the Church of the Holy Spirit—the women of the small congregation performed a dance almost identical with that of the M'deup, which reached its climax when they "spoke in tongues."

In other parts of Africa I have seen people already in trance perform dances; but even in these cases the only techniques known for inducing trance are either previous dances or what it seems simplest to call mystic and contemplation. I am not quite certain how important are the different components—the physical movement and the sound of the toms-toms—in producing this state. It very often happens that the players of the tom-toms will go into what appears to be a light trance; their eyes become glazed and unfocussed, and their bodies, except for their arms, appears completely relaxed. If they are in trance, however, it stops as soon as they stop playing, and nothing is necessary to awaken them.

From the artificial society of Senegal I want now to take you a thousand miles further east to the strange and somewhat repellent, and even more elaborate society of Dahomey. In contrast to Senegal, which had been exposed to Moslem and Christian influence for centuries, Dahomey was a completely independent native state which was only overthrown by force less than fifty years ago, and in which customs, manners, and above all the religions, which were current before the conquest, are still vivid in the native mind today. Dahomey was an absolute monarchy, with an elaborate feudal system and very complex social rules. During the whole of the nineteenth century its very name was blood-curdling to the average white man, particularly on account of the enormous quantity of human sacrifice which took place at the death of kings and at the anniversaries of their deaths. Their society is far too complex for me to discuss here; all I wish to talk about now is the religious system, and the dances which are a chief part of their worship.

The Dahomeyan religion is elaborate and complex. The basis of their theology is the creator Maou, whose symbol is the sun. He was too powerful and too abstract to be worshipped, but Maou was also a trinity; the other members were his mother, Lissa, whose symbol is the chameleon, and his son, Gou, whose symbol is the crescent moon. When Maou created the earth he created a number of lesser supernaturals, of which his mother and son were the first; and it is these lesser supernaturals which are worshipped and invoked.

I use the word fetish to describe these lesser supernaturals. I have chosen this word because it is fairly frequent in the literature, although it is somewhat obscure. Each of these supernatural forces has some object or animal in the real world which is its representative and to which, as its representative, its worshippers have to pay personal homage. Thus the principle of royal and capricious power is personified in the panther; all the servants and priests of this power have reverence for this animal. The principle of fertility and fruitfulness is symbolized by the river; the worshippers of this group have to perform a special ritual whenever they come across running water. There may be as many as fifty such fetishes in Dahomey, each with its special

28

worship and ritual and sacred object; but except for the most ignorant persons, the sacred object is only a symbol, and has no power in itself.

These different fetishes are connected with different kinship groupings, and there is no choice as to which fetish a person will worship. He or she inherits the fetish from his father or mother according to the type of marriage by which his parents were united. As soon as a woman is pregnant she consults a priest of her fetish and he finds by divination whether the child which is to be born to her is to be a servant to the fetish or not. If a child is to be a servant to the fetish, he or she spends nearly three years during his later childhood in a fetish convent during which he is instructed in the sacred language and ritual, in mystic contemplation, and in the dances which form the greatest part of the public or non-esoteric worship. Both men and women take part in these dances which are also worship, and the invocation of the supernatural principle which the dance serves. These dances form an essential, integrative rôle in the community, and assure it of the benevolence of the power which is being invoked.

These dances are both numerous and complex, and it would be impossible in the space I have here to give even a list of them. I will try, however, to describe a few of the dances connected with five of the fetishes. Even with these inadequate descriptions, I think the principle behind these dances will become clear. It is the third type of pantomime to which I referred—the imitation of the supernatural principle.

Each fetish has its own special costume for dancing, and its own particular dances; although all the dances are founded on the swinging rhythmic movement of the shoulder, yet they are so ordered as to suggest the particular qualities of the fetish they honor. Every dance in each fetish's repertoire has its proper name and sequence; there is nothing haphazard about them. The fetishers have, too, a special method of greeting the laity and their own superiors; the devotees of the thunder-fetish for instance greet their superiors by crouching and putting their joined hands between those of the fetisher, while they wave their bottoms from side to side; when they greet a layman they hold their hands down and make a thunder noise in their throat.

The Heviosso, or thunder-fetish, have three separate types of dance.

The dance of the Legba is always performed first, to avert evil spirits; for the same reason the Legba dancer always prances in front of the other performers, waving his olisbos [artificial penis] in the air. The most general dance is the gobahun, which is danced in pairs, very quick, with vehement arm movements and sudden twists. Both men and women dance this; for both, the principal item of dress is a full skirt reaching a little below the knees, in various materials, but chiefly white; and when the dancers turn suddenly, it spreads out wide like a ballet skirt.

The most dramatic of the thunder dances is the adahoun; it is danced by a very few young men naked to the waist except for a necklace of big red and blue beads, and wearing a short very full skirt about nine inches long, like a tiny tutu, tight-fitting velvet drawers reaching to the knee, and a scarf knotted under the skirt so that its ends fall down like a tail. They dance with one, or occasionally two, sossyabi—sacred axes with wooden handles and brass heads—holding the sossyabi in the mouth or the left hand. Their dance is completely wild, for they represent the destructive element of thunder; with the sossyabi in their teeth—no mean feat for it is very heavy—they rush in every direction with their hands held out and their heads jerking backwards and forwards; they are completely bacchic and frenzied, and their big-pupilled eyes are fixed on infinity. They destroy whatever comes under their hand—plants, trees, roofs, even objects sacred to the fetish. They seize what they fancy—hats and clothes off the spectators, animals and even children—shouting when they have got booty, and waving it in the air towards the tom-tom, with whom they later deposit it. So possessed are they that they roll on the ground, eat earth, turn somersaults and walk on the narrowest coping. The onlookers are in a state of pleasurable terror; the dancers are filled with the spirit of the thunder and must not be opposed in anything they are inspired to do—who can oppose a thunderbolt? They once took my topee—which alarmed me, for I had no other—but the kindly Legba returned it when the dance was finished.

On one occasion the dancers of Sagbata (the smallpox) came to pay a friendly visit to Heviosso. The devotees of Sagbata are mostly women; they are dressed in double crinolines, one longer than the other, both ending with deep fringes; across their breasts were innumerable necklaces of cowries crossing on their back; more cowries surrounded their ankles; on their arms they had plainer bracelets. The men were dressed very similarly, except that their skirts were only knee-length, and they wore embroidered hats whereas the women had headcloths.

On their first arrival they greeted the Heviosso dancers and then waited quietly at one side. Suddenly one of the men shrieked wildly and fell forward on his face; the fetish had entered them, and they commenced dancing. Their dances are short and febrile; several were very strange. One was like a Russian gopak danced backwards; another resembled flying, the sossyabi held parallel to the ground and the dance consisting of steps in the air between jumps, the feet touching the ground so little and so lightly that it was harly perceptible. From time to time one of the fetishers would start singing whatever came into his head—for instance boasting about the superiority of his magic, telling of a stolen bicycle, crying that his wife had deceived him; in fact all the symptoms of delirium.

The dancers who worship the chameleon Lissa have their clothes covered with white crosses; the men wear hats of feathers, and hold double silver bells in their hands. The dance is very quick and continuous, one dancer starting just before the other leaves off, so that there is a continual darting movement.

In the dances worshipping the snake fetish Danh, the women dance in a single file with a harmless boa on their necks. But from the esthetic point of view the most spectacular and beautiful were the dances of Nesshoué, the river. The Nesshoué are always in a very great company and elaborately dressed in many cloths of different but harmonious tones, avoiding all pure colors except blue and green. They wear chased silver daggers at their waists, and on their arms cunningly worked armlets and bracelets in solid silver; the men carrying sossyabi with the axe-like blade in silver, the women horses'-tails silver-mounted.

Their dances are mostly slow and undulating, after the character of a river; they dance together so that their varied clothing looks like a bed of living flowers, their silver ornaments sparkling like dew. Against the background of the blue sky and the palms, with occasional trees of a deeper green, and scarlet fruit, the effect is of the greatest beauty. Sometimes they dance in lines and sometimes in single file, but always with the strictest rhythm and co-ordination. There is only one dance which is done individually. Perhaps the most lovely of all their dances is the Selili, or gleaning dance—the river makes the harvest. In a lone line they hold their sossyabi and fans parallel with the ground, and with one leg stretched behind them they advance with a quick undulating movement, gradually gathering speed till they seem like a sea wave.

To the west of Dahomey lies Togoland, and then the highly developed British colony of the Gold Coast. West of the Gold Coast to the borders of Senegal lies the wildest, least developed and most primitive portion of West Africa; and it is about one portion of this—the Ivory Coast—that I now wish to speak. When I was in the Ivory Coast in 1934, it had not yet been completely subdued; some portions were still under military rule, and cannibalism was not unusual away from the single road.

For a hundred miles inward from the coast, land is covered with the densest tropical primeval forest, so thick that you are completely lost ten yards from a path, and in it Europeans have not infrequently starved to death less than a mile from their camps. Within this forest live innumerable small groups of Negroes, usually numbering only a few hundred, each with its own civilization, its own language, its own religion, and its own dances. Beyond the forest belt lies semi-open savannah and most of the agglomerations of people are larger here, and the variety of dances less. Some of the groups on the edge of the forest, however, have the most spectacular dances of all.

The Ivory Coast is one of the two chief African areas in which masked dances are found. In the last thirty years these masks have become well-known in the Western world and are, I think rightly, considered to be among the finest examples of non-European plastic art. They have evolved entirely as part of the paraphernalia of special sacred dances; they might indeed be considered dance costumes.

With practically no exceptions, the masks in West Africa are extremely sacred; in many places women and children may not look at them, and some of them are completely esoteric, and may only be seen by a few initiates. They are, many of them, of astonishing size and elaboration. The bulk is limited by the fact that they have to be carried on human heads, but many achieve a weight of sixty pounds or over. The fact that they have to be balanced means constant consideration of a balanced weight and stress, of symmetry. Some masks are literally yards high or wide; I have seen masks from the north Ivory Coast which were nearly five yards high, and at Javara in the upper Ivory Coast I myself saw masks ten feet across.

In our museums most of these masks are monochrome, but all that I saw in West Africa were colored with vegetable dyes in bright and quite arbitrary patterns. These dyes are impermanent and have to be constantly repainted. The masks are always representations of real objects or of concepts; but these are so highly stylized that they are often almost completely unrecognizable. For example, in Javara the vulture mask consisted of two enormous beaks, each about four feet long, joined in the center by a tiny little Janus figure. This mask was painted red, white, and black, and I should have thought it completely abstract if an interpreter had not explained it to me.

The masks are considered solid magic, totally imbued with the spirit of the supernatural. When the dancer puts on the mask he becomes a supernatural, and for that reason it is always stated that nobody knows who the wearer of the mask is. In a smaller village where everybody can be recognized by a dozen peculiarities, such a statement is literally absurd; but to the Africans it is meaningful, for though they know that a man is absent they do not know who is under the mask, for the possessing spirit can completely transform the masked dancer into his own likeness. This possibility is increased by the fact that with masked dancers the whole body is covered with the exception of the hands and feet. Most of the masks have holes through which heavy raffia coverings can be suspended; and nearly always the whole body of the dancer is covered in this way so that the masked dancers look like haystacks walking. Incidentally, it may be remarked that African masks are worn over the forehead and not, as with us, over the face. This means that masks are meant to be seen at an angle of about thirty degrees out of the upright and from below; seen thus, many of the apparent distortions in African carving disappear.

Masked dancers are the most spectacular element of West African dancing; they are also, from the point of view of dancing, almost the least interesting. The chief reason for this seems to be the fact that the dancer is so overburdened by his mask and costume that he can hardly move. The sacredness of the role he is impersonating may also possibly restrain his movements. In any event, most masked dancers do little more than shuffle about with a sort of syncopated trot. Some do not even do that. The masks of the Niabois with the accompanying heavy costume of raffia look like nightmare caricatures of the Empress Eugénie, and they are so clumsy that they have to be led about by two keepers.

Only twice did I see some masked dancers whose dance had any considerable interest. One of these was among the Goro in the deepest forest. The Goro are, incidentally, notorious cannibals. A young man had been accidentally killed in a hunting accident in the forest, and his body had been brought home for mourning and burial. In the early dawn of the day before he was going to be buried, all the gods of the forest came to receive his soul. A slow and solemn procession of animal masks surmounting mountains of grass came loping in from the forest, crowded into the dead man's hut, and stooped over him, and then one

33

by one came into the open place outside and made swirling pirouettes so that their robes of grass flew out like a three-dimensional ballet skirt. After the funeral, similar dancing was performed unmasked by the near relatives. These dancers were naked except for a very small loin-cloth and thick anklets of monkey fur. They held a piece of cotton in their hands like a Spanish bull fighter's cape, and performed extraordinary acrobatics as they twisted it.

The other spectacular masked dance was that which took place at Javara in the savannah. This dance was of very considerable significance, and consisted in the ritual killing of totemic animals. The dancers were about a dozen masked men, one for each totem-group, and a master of the masks. The orchestra consisted of a number of very thin narrow drums beaten with curved canes, and several flute-like instruments. Besides perfectly enormous and very lovely masks—highly stylized, and colored red, white, and black—the masked dancers were dressed in loose raffia pyjamas colored brown and black, very bulky; attached to the mask was a mop of brown raffia, falling over the head and shoulders to the waist. The masked men carried two long, pointed sticks which they used somewhat after the manner of ski-sticks, making enormous jumps with them; these sticks had a band of metal jangles round the middle. The master of the masks was naked except for a tiny flesh-colored loin-cloth; he continually smothered himself with dust so that he looked dazzlingly white.

Each masked dancer performed in turn; and while he danced, all the onlookers belonging to that totem-clan reproduced his gestures with tiny unconscious movements. The stork or the crocodile (or whatever animal it might be) would come out from his quarter very proud and haughty, jumping about and waving his sticks; everybody nearby would be terrified and run away from him, except the orchestra and the master of the masks, who followed him and egged him on. As no one dared approach him, the mask became more superb and wild, doing the strangest acrobatic feats and waving his head backwards and forwards, the master of the masks encouraging him with gesture and pantomime. At last his movements became so uncontrolled that he fell to the ground, literally dazed. Then the master of the masks would go through the appropriate pantomime of stalking and killing the animal, and would take away his sticks, which he gave to the orchestra; and all the little children of that totem would run at the fallen masker and pull tufts off his clothes, and then would lead him crestfallen back to his quarter.

This pantomime was gone through with every mask in turn until only the master of the masks was left. This man was a dancer of extraordinary ingenuity and technique; for the three hours during which the ceremony went on he danced continually, sometimes dramatically, and sometimes in a burlesque fashion, making wicked mockery of Mohammedans and Christians at their worship, of soldiers and hunters, of different animals. He had a great command of expressive gesture, and could communicate over a considerable distance the various moods or people he was miming. He had a command of stage technique raised to a pitch of virtuosity which I have never seen equalled by a professional dancer.

The only semi-sacred dance that I saw which employed masks was a hunting dance, also in the Ivory Coast forest. There were only three performers, two hunters armed with bows and arrows and knives, and an antelope. The antelope was danced by a boy about fifteen, with a small antelope mask, realistic except that it was painted purple; it was attached to his head with a piece of dappled material under it which covered his face and body; a straw tail was attached to one end of it and he had the usual jangles on his legs. His knees were permanently bent and his body held forward, so that he was able to see the ground under the cloth which fell away from his face; but the mask was so placed that the antelope seemed to be looking upwards all the time. The hunters stuck a tuft of grass attached to a stake in the middle of an open piece of ground, and then crouched in cover among the bushes and people surrounding it. The antelope came forward very timidly, sniffing the air, and starting at every tiny sound and shadow; one of the hunters moved so that his knife made a sound, and the antelope scampered off out of sight. It came back very cautiously, scurrying from shadow to shadow, until it arrived again at the open place.

Suddenly it saw the planted grass, stiffened and then made towards it; a few yards from it, it was overcome with timidity and hurried to cover. This scene was repeated several times; the grass looked so tempting, but there was something wrong with the smell, and the position was too exposed. At last greed got the better of caution, and the antelope sidled up to the grass, acting as though it had no intention of touching it; suddenly, when it was opposite, it darted towards it, and at the same moment the two hunters pulled their bows. The antelope was badly wounded but it was able to stagger a few paces away; then it suddenly collapsed on its side, moved its arms and legs meaninglessly, quivered and lay still. The hunters came out of their cover and cut off the straw tail with their knives. The pantomime was most exquisitely observed and acted. It seemed spontaneous, but could hardly be so, for the rhythm of the drums and rhumba rattles was carefully observed.

A sort of variant of the masked dancing is the dancing of dead men which is found throughout all this region. The dances are somewhat similar, but the dead man has no wooden mask; his face is covered with cloth which is usually blank, and no single portion of the skin is allowed to show. Sometimes beneath the cloth face-covering the "dead men" carry whistles which give out a very ghostly hooting noise. These dances are less sacred than the mask dances, and seem to be used to quite an extent to discipline children.

It is in the Ivory Coast too that are found most of the group dances which pantomime the emotion which the dancers are meant to feel later—above all, war dances, and religious dances. Unfortunately these dances though most beautiful to watch are almost impossible to describe. I could give you the details of their often beautiful costumes, and could try to suggest the effect which these dances produce. But it is really as impossible to talk about these dances as it is to describe a classical ballet—although choreographers have a language for doing just that. They are miracles of frenzied rhythmic motion, most complicated and controlled, an ordered savagery which I am not facile enough to describe, although the dancers are able to learn and remember the steps. About the best of these dances it is not possible to be patronizing; they can only be judged by the highest standards of choreography; and by these standards, the war dances of the Dapango or Baule—with their precision and extravagant movements, seem to me to be in the same category as one of my favorite ballets, the Polovtsian dances from "Prince Igor." I feel, however, that I can really say no more about these pure dances than I did in the generalizations with which I began.

This region is, as I have already said, overwhelmingly rich in its variety of dances. Out of the whole number I will describe two which have a sufficient scenario to make a description feasible. The first dance took place somewhat north of the forest in a little riverside village by moonlight. Additional light was given by piles of burning straw. The music consisted entirely of drums, starting very slowly and working up with a gradual crescendo to almost unbearable speed, rather like the second act of the "Sacre du Printemps." It was the most rigidly formal dance I saw in Africa.

The dance opened with a young boy holding a long stick to the end of which was attached a small white pennant; he went round the dancing space very slowly several times, waiving his flag in every direction, and then retired. He returned followed by two young men dressed in white shirts and drawers, each carrying standing on his shoulders a little girl aged about six, dressed in a flaxen wig, red coat covered with cowries and glass and little bells and long blue trousers. These were followed by an old witch naked to the waist and dressed in a white pagne, holding a sinisterly empty calabash in her hand which she waved towards the dancers all the time. Also, during the whole dance the flag-bearer circled round the dancers.

At first the little girls waved their arms and heads rhythmically, while the young men bore them round the circle, doing a complicated and syncopated step with their feet. But as the rhythm mounted the little girls lost the perpendicular position; they hung upside down and were thrown about as if they were dolls; they seemed jointless, but their hands and heads still marked the rhythm. At last the climax was reached; suddenly and very violently the little girls were thrown toward the tom-toms, held by the ankles at arm's length, and were then swung in circles till they almost touched the ground. Just before they actually touched it, they were suddenly lifted completely limp, and carried away over the young men's shoulders upside down. The witch followed, carefully holding her empty calabash as if it were overflowing; last of all went the standard-bearer, still swirling his flag. The drum beats died away.

Finally I am going to describe a dance which we were very lucky to see, since it only took place once a year on the night of the first rains, and we accidentally arrived at the village in the southeast Ivory Coast the night that the threatening storm had called up the dancers. The moon was nearly full but it was often obscured by clouds, and the illumination was fitful. The dance took place on a very large piece of bare ground in front of the village, which may have been a prepared field; a large assortment of drums grouped in the center. The first group of dancers was about a score of young men, naked except for a most exiguous loin-cloth and garters; they held rattles in their hands. They started dancing fairly close to the tom-toms, making a small circle; each time a round was completed, the steps—always elaborate and complicated—were varied. The rest of the population stood around in a large circle, singing some sort of chant to which the dancers replied.

Gradually these onlookers added themselves to the dancing ring, first the older men, then the older women, then the young women, and finally little children who could barely toddle, but who could dance with perfect rhythm. Except for the original young men, the dancers did not indulge in a variety of steps, but followed with a sort of syncopated shuffle, singing loudly. The score of dancers became more and more ecstatic, doing increasingly complicated steps, cart-wheels, forward somersaults and so on. When there were no onlookers except us, and the circle of dancers was right on the boundary of the field, a number of strangely dressed old men ran out into the center. The light was too bad to be able to make out the details of their costumes, but they showed a very odd silhouette.

They held cymbals in their hands, and had different whistles in their mouths, and in turn they went through an exceedingly realistic and well observed pantomime of the copulation of various beasts and birds. Each man represented a different animal, and his whistle had a more or less appropriate note. These dances were extraordinarily impressive and serious; the old men mimed so well that they almost became goats, or cocks, or bulls before our eyes, the movements were so essential that the body which made them seem unimportant.

When all had finished they made a ring around the drums, and then four little girls, naked except for a necklace of red seeds and a tiny apron, broke through the ring of dancers, approximately from the four quarters of the compass. Very slowly and seriously they danced their way to the center, keeping exact time with one another. They danced almost squatting on the ground, holding their tiny aprons in one hand, and scattering imaginary seeds with the other; they progressed with a sort of zig-zag, a few steps to the right, then as many to the left. They arrived in front of the old men together and knelt on the ground; and each old man blessed them in turn, laying both hands on their heads. Four of them then picked up the little girls and carried them off on their shoulders out of the ring. During all this time the big ring of dancers had been circling and singing, shouting loudly after each clap of thunder. As the storm got nearer, they shouted louder and louder, until suddenly the first drops of rain fell; the dancers broke the ring and rushed to the tom-toms, and with the drummers at the head the whole group returned to the village in a mass.

I hope that through using—and though using—the unsatisfactory medium of words I have been able to give you some impression of the enormous scope and importance of the dance in West Africa. From the esthetic point of view the dance is undoubtedly the chief African art; all the other arts, music, singing, sculpture, textiles, and lesser handicrafts have been diverted to serve and enhance the dance. From a religious point of view it is hardly less important; the West Africans worship their gods, control the dangerous forces of nature, and call down divine power into themselves by dancing. Finally, the dance has important social functions. The group of warriors and initiates assert their unity by dancing together. Crime is controlled by the witch-finding trance-dance which discovers criminals, and the chief moments when the more primitive groups gather together is when they are all watching some of their number dance for the whole community. For most of us the dance is essentially one of the pleasurable arts, used above all for relaxation; for the West Africans the dance is the chief medium which gives meaning to their lives and unites them with the forces which people their universe.

Discussion:

(GEOFFREY GORER, in response to questions:) The amount of rehearsal varies with the fetish; dancers of the higher fetishes have three years of training before performing. Warrior dancers train for about six months. The emphasis is on tradition, not creation. In an acrobatic sense, the more difficult the movement the better; there are virtuosi, though all dancers must be able to perform amazing feats. The method of training is trial and error, like that of an athlete. The dancer is shown and asked to do the same. Dancers of various fetishes are supported by community tithes and gifts, warrior dancers by their families. Sorcery dances are used for therapy and policing, and like the activity of the medicine man are used according to the amount of sickness and misfortune. There may be new dances, but lacking formal history, their age is unknown. Music and dance are inseparable, one never being used without the other. The best dancers come from the smaller, hunting tribes. In the larger, agricultural tribes dance diminishes in importance and vitality. Large movements typical in both dance and everyday gesture.

Dance and Dance-Drama in Haiti

BY HAROLD COURLANDER

T HE Republic of Haiti is the earliest state governed constitu-
tionally by Negroes. Its original inhabitants were Indians, almost all of whom were slaughtered or worked to death in the
search for gold. Negro slaves were imported during the sixteenth,
seventeenth, and eighteenth centuries from West and perhaps East
Africa. Because of white tyranny, the Negro slaves revolted in 1804
and massacred the whites. They have been self-governing since. At
present Haiti is ninety percent Negro and the rest mulatto, and has a
population of three and one half to four million people. Haiti shares its
island with Santo Domingo, which has half as large a population and
occupies twice as much land. The Haitians speak a language known as
Creole, which is a mixture of Norman, Breton, and modern French,
plus West African dialects, Spanish, and some Portugese and English.

The occupation of the people varies with the region in which they
live. Those in the large plains are likely to be cane-cutters and
plantation laborers. On the smaller plains, where the large corpora-
tions have not acquired land, the men are likely to have farms. The
higher you go in the hills, the smaller these farms get, till finally they
are gardens, nestling in tiny pockets wherever earth and moisture will
cling together. In the coastal villages, the people are fishermen. Where
natural clay beds lie, they are potters. Mostly, however, the men and
women of Haiti are peasants. They live in white plastered wattle huts
roofed with grass, and they till the hillsides or the river banks for coffee,
cotton, melons, yams, and other tropical produce.

It should be pointed out that Haiti is bi-cultural. The so-called élite
or upper class from which comes most of Haiti's presidents, legislators,
large businessmen, public office-holders, army officers, and other
representatives of the money class hew rigidly to the line of French

tradition. The differences between the cultural patterns of the élite and the peasantry need not be gone into here, since the money class is—naturally—comparatively tiny and, to our way of thinking, unimportant in a consideration of Haitian customs. Whatever the economic and social forces at bottom, it is the peasantry who give Haiti its uniqueness and distinction. Any general reference to Haitian people that I may make has in mind the farmers, laborers, peasants, fishermen, and potters, who make up perhaps ninety-five percent or more of the population.

In contrast to certain eastern peoples, let us say the Javanese, and even the Africans, Haitians are characterized in their ways by gross, direct movements, and lack of decorative motifs. Outwardly the Haitian is a simple and straightforward utilitarian. The things he makes with his hands serve a vital physical purpose. They help him to work, or make him comfortable; nothing more. A chair is made to sit on, a mortar to pound grain in, a basket to carry in. Decoration is conspicuous by its absence, with some special exceptions. Carved wooden utensils are as plain and simple as the human mind can conceive them. The clay pottery, until recently, was distinctive in its lack of decoration, and in the small number of variations in design. The game board on which wari, the African "checker" game, is played is devoid not only of decoration, but even of legs to hold it steady and of the usual extra pockets to hold pieces acquired from the opponent. The gambling game called mayamba is played, not with specially made chips, but with bits of broken plates. Two pieces of iron struck together are an adequate substitute for a sonorous bell. Only the barest essentials of everything are present.

The finer motifs are absent not only in objects, but also in movement. Where the Balinese lays stress on the pose of the hands and fingers, the Haitian stresses, say, the position of the arm. The Balinese sense of poised balance is absent in Haiti, and in its place there is an attitude of frontal assault against natural laws, such as gravity, and a tendency toward the acrobatic. Acrobatic in the meaning that one works against nature, making the movement the hard way. It is as true in the lifting of a heavy object and in the wielding of a hoe as it is in the dance in Haiti. There is almost always a feeling of solidity in Haitian posture. One has the impression of closeness between the earth and the human body. Lightness in the dance is sometimes seen, but it is thus defined only in relation to other Haitian movements. If Haitian movement lacks the more delicate and decorative elements, it does possess strength. And the broader and grosser movements can be beautiful too.

For the largest part of the Haitian people, dancing is an act deeply rooted in almost all of the important events of life, beginning perhaps with the christening of a child, and continuing beyond the individual's death. There is secular and religious dancing, and dancing that falls indefinitely between the two. People dance to supplicate the countless Afro-Haitian loa, or spirits, to accompany the making of magic to ward off devils and demons, to send the dead on their way with encouragement, and in honor of ancestors and twins. Sometimes they dance because a loa has taken possession of their bodies. They dance to make work easy, to celebrate the building of a new house, or to welcome a guest. There are few gatherings, religious or secular, that do not begin or end with dancing. Music and movement are so closely related that they nearly always occur together. Wherever there is music, there is dancing. In religious service both are expressions of supplication.

Among the work gangs in the fields, a drummer or trumpeter incites the laborers to a rhythm of work which essentially constitutes a dance. I believe Haitians are intensely dance-conscious—which is an inverse way of saying it, inasmuch as dance is so thoroughly taken for granted by them that they are unconscious of its being something separate from their lives. Singing, drumming, and dance movement are, in a way, integral; they are parts of one whole. One hears the Haitian say: "tambou' ça yo chante,'" meaning "the drums are singing," or "tambou' ça yo danse,'" "the drums are dancing." There is a vague element of magic in dance, too. Dance is a positive statement of life. It sets forces into motion. It is not only expressive, but creative. It has powers to cure and vitalize, to appease and to aggravate, to satisfy and discover. Small wonder that many uprisings and revolts of the slaves during the eighteenth century were born in surreptitious dances at remote places in the mountains and plains.

Music and dancing in Haiti largely follow African tradition, with the exception of some forms that will be mentioned later. The drumming appears to utilize West African techniques, and the singing tends toward the responsory form, in which a single leader sings one or more lines, and then another individual or a chorus responds with one or more lines, alternately. The melodies range from French to African, but the methods of using them are mainly African. Occasionally there is an overlapping of lines in responsory singing, which appears to be an approved West African procedure.

Not only the musical methods but the devices themselves often follow and conform to an African pattern, so that one finds the ancestral forms—not too far removed—of Haitian musical instruments in West

43

and Central Africa. Usually there are drums of either Dahomey or Congo patterns, in various combinations, depending on what dance is involved. The dancing typically takes place in a court adjoining a building; this court is covered with a canopy of leaves or grass, and is open on three sides. A center pole, supporting the middle portion of the canopy, usually holds one or more oil lamps. The dancers move around this central pole in a counter-clockwise direction in numbers ranging from two to perhaps a hundred or more.

This center pole, called a po'teau (or po'teau mitan), is a significant "prop" in the drama and meaning of Haitian dancing. Down this pole the loa (spirits) come when they enter the gathering. Down this pole comes the drum-spirit, too, to enter into the head and sticks of the drums. At the foot of the po'teau sacrifices are laid out, and maize flour paintings made. In the topmost parts of the pole protective household gardes, or fetiches, may be suspended, and in its branches may be hidden stone celts sacred to certain loa. Around this pole the dance characteristically takes place. Many of the postures of the dancers are strikingly African. They have feet flat on the ground, and slightly bent knees, flexed backs with the buttocks and shoulders thrust to the rear, or sometimes the shoulders and head pushed far forward. The singing leader is usually a woman, and the dancers do the singing. Spectators sit or stand around the edges of the dance court.

There are many secular dances that take place in such settings as this: Pinyique, Pastorelle, Ciyé, Chica, Ti Crip, Mangouline, Zesse, Raboto, Mascaron, Malfini, and many more. The rhythms are generally distinct, the drum orchestras variously constituted, and the steps and postures different in some cases, similar in others. All of these are simple bamboches, or good-time social dances. Around the dance courts one encounters women with trays selling refreshments, tables at which card and dice games flourish, and perhaps in some corner the chip-flipping gambling game called mayamba. There is often much cheap rum and tafia flowing at a penny or two a glass, and in quarters near the cities and plantations there are usually a number of prostitutes present.

A dance called the Méringue, referred to by élite Haitians as the "Haitian national dance," is European in character; its postures, gestures, and movements being based upon the Haitian peasant's concept of European dancing. It always struck me as being an unconscious burlesque of either the richer classes or of European dancing, but it is only fair to mention that I had the same impression in watching the élite dance the Méringue. The shoulders are held very stiff and straight, the face impassive and inscrutable, and there is considerable hip-movement. The music for the Méringue is provided by drums, tambourines, guitars, and marimbas. Among the élite these would be replaced by pianos, trumpets, violins, clarinets, and whatever else is available. Other secular dances follow European rather than African patterns too, as noted in G. E. Simpson's "Peasant Songs and Dances of Northern Haiti," in the Journal of Negro History for April 1940.

Among the African-type dances are many associated with work. There is the ordinary night dance of the société, or agricultural work-group. During certain hours of the day the members of the group are in the fields, weeding or harvesting, and in the evening they gather at the house of the man whose land they are working. They are fed well, and subsequently the drummers of the société begin to play, and the men begin to dance. If they are a société Congo, there are dances connected with the traditions of the Congo cults; if they are a société Rada, they may dance any one of a dozen steps connected to the Rada cult traditions. The men may sleep on the grounds of the host if they live far off, and in this case they march and dance to the fields of another member of the group the next morning, led by drummers or players of conch shell trumpets. There is a similar festival held after a communal house-building party, the dance here being called the Bamboula.

In most parts of Haiti wakes are the occasion for rather simple, though gay, dances. While the older relatives and neighbors sit inside the house with the family of the deceased, the younger people gather outside under the canopy adjoining the building to sing, tell stories, and dance. It is believed that such gaiety is pleasing to the soul of the dead person. Some of these dances involve moving in a circle around a hat on the ground, to the accompaniment of singing and handclapping, as in the Mexican hat dance. Sometimes there is a stick dance, each participant holding a baton which he strikes against that of the person on each side. Some of the dancers move clockwise, some counter-clockwise, all hitting their sticks with great precision. There is much reversing and backtracking, and at certain times the dancers all crouch on their heels, continuing to strike with their batons.

Nine or ten days following the burial of a dead person, there are more rites in his honor, and more dancing. On the habitation of the family there will be dancing of the Juba or Martinique, which is specially reserved for such occasions. Every few years a family may give a feast for the dead (mangé morts), and here again the Juba or other steps will be danced. The music for the Juba dance is provided by a single drum with a goatskin head. It is played in a horizontal position, the drummer sitting astride it and striking with his hands, modulating the tones with the heels of his bare feet. A second musician beats hard sticks against the wooden body of the drum. On the whole it is a dance for the older people rather than the younger, though I have seen even children participating.

The foregoing dances are encountered from one end of the year to the other. But each spring, in the few weeks preceding Easter, there is a great secular dance celebration called Rara, or Lwalwadi. It is built around the Christian holidays, but beyond that there is nothing familiar about it, and it is not clear just when or how this festival originated. Some Haitians claim the origin to be African rites, though the symbolism has become adulterated, while other Haitians say they can remember the time when Rara was not known in certain regions of the Republic. It may be possible that the general idea came from Cuba, where there are pre-Easter celebrations known as Comparsas, and where the Dahomeyan tribal designation, Arada, becomes Arara—though this is sheer hazard. In any case, the Emperor Soulouque officially recognized the festival nearly a hundred years ago, and picked a "King of Lwalwadi" to preside over it.

There are musicians who play drums and bamboo or shell trumpets, and bearers of flags, paper shields, and torches. Behind them come the dancers, who may be members of a work-group société or simply men, women, and children who have gathered at the sound of music. With a kind of drum-major in the lead, the musicians move down the country roads, the dancing throng pressing at their heels. In Port-au-Prince there are countless bands competing for attention, and they may number as many as a hundred dancers in each, though most are considerably smaller. On one country road I once saw a Rara group that must have had at least five hundred dancers. They jammed the road from side to side, and were strung out for a great distance. Such bands, under many names, move from one compound or village to another, stopping to serenade while their chiefs extend decorated money baskets on long bamboo poles for donations. Often they feature not only music, but skilled professional dancers and jugglers, usually not more than one or two in a band.

These professional dancers—male, except in the case of young children—range in age from four or five to more than fifty. Their costumes are brilliant and ornate; they wear headdresses of flowers, mirrors, and towering antlers; also brightly colored shirts sparkling with beads, foil, and other decorative objects. During this pre-Easter period, bands of costumed maypole dancers roam the streets of the towns and cities. Dressed as women, the performers are all men. Here, too, the money basket on the end of a pole is passed to spectators. Costumed stick dancers (again men dressed as women) compete for the attention and contributions of onlookers. But most of the dancing is done by the unorganized and unprofessional population. Women going to or returning from market join the Rara groups, dancing for miles in their wake, sometimes with heavy baskets on their heads. These are riotous dances, with much symbolic license and overt sexual gesture. Shocked observers in former years attributed Haiti's dense population to its Rara festivities.

I have seen fragments of several rather curious acrobatic dances. One was a pantomime of a wrestling match, another of prize-fighting; both of them clearly dance in every sense. On one occasion at a Saturday night gathering I saw a man performing an erotic dance while standing on his head. This last has, I think, been reported by another observer in Haiti.

Probably the most interesting of the Haitian dances, and the most complex, are associated with cults and religious rituals. It will be worth while, I think, to give a brief picture of the background of these cults and their beliefs. The religious patterns of the Arada of Dahomey, of the Nago (or Yoruba) of Nigeria, and of certain Congo peoples, seem to have survived transplanting to the New World, while customs and beliefs of other West African nations appear to have been absorbed into these major Haitian cults or to have disappeared altogether. Perhaps the outstanding characteristics of the Dahomean religious system were a supreme being called Maou (or Mawu-Lissa) and a pantheon of spirit beings called vodouns. Such spirit beings, occasionally referred to as deities or gods, are identified with various forces of nature—with thunder and lightning, the curative powers of herbs and medicines, the sea, the river, the crossroads (which are very important to the West African), the cemetery, and so on. The neighboring Nigerian Nago possessed a similar pantheon of spirit beings, called orishas, which, structurally at least, resembled that of the Dahomeans. In Haiti today, the Nago system has been fused into the Dahomean, and this cult is called Vodoun.

There are perhaps thousands of spirit-beings designated as loa, whose essential characteristics are those of the Dahomean vodouns, and whose personalities and propensities have been modified by several centuries in a new world. A great representation of the Nago orishas and the Dahomean vodouns is present in Haiti, and in addition to the older gods there are many new ones of apparently pure Haitian origin. Moreover, there is an infiltration of the Christian system, so that saints and other biblical figures take their places among the loa, and the Christian god becomes the ultimate source of all things. The loa swell their numbers further by recruiting from a special category of the dead, in a similar manner to our saints. There are other aspects of Vodoun, such as special reverence for, and worship of, the dead, with special attention being paid to twins, albinos, etc.

The Congo or Guinée cult, or cluster of cults, appears to have a system comparable to Vodoun, although the pantheon of spirit-beings is distinct. There are both benevolent and malevolent deities, with a seemingly endless variety of personalities. In the north of Haiti this constellation of beliefs and dances is generically called Congo, in the south, Pétro.

The spirit-beings do not function as abstractions. They enter and take possession of the bodies of the people who serve them. The Haitians say the loa "mount" them or "ride" them, or "enter one's head." When they sing that a loa arrives, it usually means that his presence is manifested by the possession or trance of one or more persons in the gathering. Let us say there is a Vodoun dance at someone's house, attended by relatives and close friends. The ceremonial occasion may be the christening of a set of new drums, after which the evening is devoted to singing and dancing. This is a religious event. Sometimes the distinction between religious and profane dancing is vague, but I believe the test is one of the attitude involved. Here there is an attitude of supplication, and an awareness of supernatural forces and spirit-beings.

The full distinction is hard to make. The gathering may have many of the earmarks of a purely social gathering, which of course it is in large part. But the dance steps are different. There is a sense of discipline. There is authority. The po'teau or centerpole is far more significant than in secular dancing. The dancers move close to it. It is the entrance way of the loa. Perhaps a drummer will come forward from the drummers' bench to touch his instrument against the pole, calling it to the attention of the vague force known as the hountor, spirit of the drums.

Suddenly, while the dance is in progress, one of the participants staggers and lurches from side to side. He has been "mounted" by his loa. His eyes take on a fixed look, or perhaps the lids close. In this trance condition he may continue to dance, the other performers moving aside to grant him the right of way. If he becomes violent, the other dancers remove themselves from the court altogether, leaving it to the possessed person, for in his head the spirit-being resides. For the moment he is the spirit-being by extension, since his every action is directed by the loa who "rides" him. The things he does are characteristic of his loa. Even strangers who do not know this man personally may be able to identify his loa by his behavior. The drums continue to beat, usually not stopping until the spirit has been pacified in some way.

Perhaps a great many persons will be entered and ridden by spirit-beings during an evening. These possessions are not simply ecstatic seizures. Most of them have well-defined meanings. A person who is mounted for the first time is apt to be violent and irresponsible. The Vodoun priest or an assistant must control the spirit or it will do damage to the mounted person or to others. Having evoked and allowed hysterical manifestations of this intensity, it is necessary to control them, and the "wild spirit" is identified and baptized by the Vodoun priest, who then removes it from the possessed person's head. On subsequent visitations the loa is less and less violent, and a time comes when the devotee—who by now can probably be described as acting half by memory and half by fraud—follows a highly formalized pattern of activity when the loa "mounts" him.

There is a spirit by the name of Legba in the Haitian pantheon. He was and is known among the Yoruba and the Dahomean peoples of West Africa as a messenger of the gods, an interpreter, an intervener for humans, and the personification of accident. He was not a spirit in quite the same sense as the other vodouns and orishas, but he was tremendously important. He was a fertility fetish, guardian of the crossroads, protector of the doorway or gateway, and a phallic god. In Haiti Legba is one of the big spirit-beings, and, as in Africa, he is the first of the deities appealed to in a religious service. When a person is mounted by this loa one of the things he may do is to go about limping, since Legba is thought of as an old man with one lamed leg, just as our priapic devil is endowed by tradition with one twisted "goat's" leg. Sometimes a person mounted by this deity may dance or spin around with a kind of cane-crutch called a Legba-stick, around which he twines his leg. Under conditions of possession, the spinning and twirling often becomes a true acrobatic feat. It occurs to me that this Legba stick may be a Haitian development of the phallic stick, or olisbos, used by Legba fetish dancers in West Africa, whom Mr. Gorer has described in "Africa Dances."

There is another loa called Gèdé, identified with the cemetery and considered a dead spirit. There are numerous conceptions of this spirit—many versions of Gèdé, and all of them are brothers. I shall quote a description of a Gèdé dance from my own book, "Haiti Singing": The floor area was not seven feet square, but there were at least twelve people crowded there, and others clustered in the doorway trying to see. Ritual flags leaned against the wall . . . A tiny place in the center of the floor remained for the Houngan, whose possession was the occasion for the service.

He was dressed in a black stovepipe hat, blue blouse with white polka dots, black shirt over black trousers, and he carried a walking stick. He smoked a pipe constantly. In the small space in the center of the floor the Houngan or Gèdé Nimbo danced. He had become, to all appearances, another person, the loa Gèdé. His voice was changed, his postures, his mannerisms, his entire personality. He spoke only through his nose, for that is the way Gèdé talks; the effect was that of a cleft palate or a harelip. He whirled around and around, singing, talking "language"; his hounsi sang, led by the houngenicon with a rattle:

"Gèdé-vi ya wè ago-é!
Gèdé-vi ya wè!
Popa Gèdé c'est loa!"

Gèdé was the center of all eyes. Most of the time he danced alone, gyrating recklessly in his tiny space. Sometimes he danced with his houngénicon. Those who watched sang and kept the rhythm with their hands . . .

Many of the loa have animal forms as well as human, and therefore persons mounted by them may mimic the movements and sounds of such animals. A man possessed by the loa Damballa, which has the form of a snake, may fall to the ground and move about the dance-court with writhing snake-like motions. Persons mounted by the loa of Bambarra, the sea-crab, assume crab-like crouching positions. A loa called Chébo entered a woman at one ceremony I observed, whereupon she attacked a freshly killed goat with a machete and then danced about in a frenzy, a piece of raw and bleeding meat between her teeth. Dr. Herskovits believes from this description that Chébo could be the tiger spirit, the Dahomean word for tiger being Sébo. Individuals possessed by Agasu, the panther, may emulate his ways with feline movements. And when Aganman, the chameleon, enters a person's head, he may assume lizard-like postures and gestures. Naturally, unless one is willing to accept the objective reality of loa as literal fact, these remarkable similarities between the actions of the possessed persons and the character of the possessing loa may seem formalized dance movements and not entirely unconscious. Or the possessing loa may be recognized strictly by the actions of the individual "ridden," or "mounted," leaving a certain amount of identification to the spectators.

Animal mimicry in religious dancing in Haiti is clearly not as specialized as in West Africa. But there is one significant survival of West African dance techniques in the southern Haitian mountains. Mr. Gorer has mentioned the use of sticks in the hands of West African animal dancers to simulate front legs. Certain Haitian religious dances require the participants to carry such sticks, which are touched to the ground as extensions of arms, thus representing forefeet.

While the general pattern of activity during possession follows in a limited tradition, there is much individual variation and improvisation. Possession constitutes a rich source of drama for the cult people. Mounted persons, or "horses" as they are sometimes called, may dance, harangue the crowd, conduct monologues in so-called "African" tongues, and indulge in pantomime, mimicry, or impersonation of the loa who ride them. An interesting question arises as to the state of mind of "possessed" persons—whether they are actually in trance or not. While I am apparently not qualified to discuss the phenomenon of possession scientifically, I believe that most of the seizures are genuine. Persons who obviously are pretending to be mounted are easily detected by the community and are considered to be acting in extremely bad taste, inasmuch as their pretense carries an implication that the loa really do not exist or have no power to possess people, and that the whole thing is an exhibitionist and fraudulent—or, at best, slightly hysterical—formality. On the other hand, certain ordeals are undergone only when the participants are in a hypnotic or trance state. The boiling pot ceremony—part of rites to initiate members into higher ranks within the cult—requires the dipping of hands into boiling oil. Persons mounted by certain spirits eat large quantities of hot red peppers that are normally not comfortably edible, and even rub them in their eyes without expressing any discomfort. When the spirit Adjasou comes in, a man may eat broken glass. When the god of iron and war enters a man's head, he may pick up bars of red-hot metal and walk in the hot coals of a fire. From such ordeals they seem to emerge unscathed, although to skeptical minds it may seem somewhat unlikely that anyone can, without preparation or trickery, handle boiling or red hot materials and not be burned.

Dr. Herskovits and Dr. Eaton have suggested the possibility that "possession" has a compensatory function; that in some cases the personality traits projected during possession are contrary to the normal personalities of the possessed people. Thus—as in drunkenness in our own society—a usually mild and quiet man may become violent and aggressive when "mounted." In addition to its dramatic and religious import, possession may therefore also be significant as a more direct outlet for repressions and frustrations, as witness the fact that earlier possessions are likely to be more violent than later ones, the repressed tensions having been somewhat relaxed by the early ones. A Haitian psychiatrist visiting the Children's Psychiatric Ward at Bellevue was very much interested in the use of dance for therapy. He said that he was convinced that the Vodoun rituals and dances are used as group psycho-therapy among the Haitians and that the Vodoun priests are aware of its value—it will be remembered that the priests control and condition the violent ecstatic actions of persons "mounted" for the first time, "identifying" the loa and diminishing its power by baptism and other social controls of the possessed individual.

One might say that the many religious dances have, roughly, all essential characteristics in common. But there are differences between the more than fifteen types, of which some are called by West African or place names. One stately dance, the Jenvalo, in which the older people and higher functionaries of the cult participate, is characterized by a "low back", the men resting their hands on their knees and the women holding their skirts. These apparently are special postures of supplication, the very word "jenvalo" being Dahomean for praise or supplication, and the dance being the most important of all supplication dances, which would tend, I believe, to prove my point.

The instruments providing music for the dances are mainly percussion. Drums are the most important of all, and the most commonly used. Stamping tubes may provide music where drums are not available. They are lengths of bamboo, varying in tone, which are struck against hard-packed earth or against a solid log. Sometimes the earth-bow, or mosquito-drum, is danced to. It is a very primitive device consisting of a single string, a bowed stick, and a hole in the ground for a sound chamber. In the Rara dances bamboo or conch trumpets are used, and in some of the Congo cult dances drums and bamboo trumpets are used together. Virtually every dance has a rattle, played by the singing leader.

The relationship of the music and the dancing is vital. One might say that the drum rhythms depend upon the songs, and the dance steps upon drum rythms. While theoretically the dancer follows the drums, actually the drumming may be affected by the motion and postures of the dancer, a kind of translation into musical rhythm of the visible movement in the dance court. Since time is kept by the singing leader with the rattle, who is also a dancer, the drummers have little choice but to follow any increase in dance tempo or intensity. In certain Nago and Dahomean dances there may be a gradual but decided acceleration before the end of the dance, the drums sometimes being directly responsible for this, driving the dancers, causing the dance to take a violent turn by the nature of their beating.

Certain signals in the rhythmic patterns cause a djaillé, or "excitement." Some of the dancers may lurch from side to side, regaining balance just short of a fall, others may leap stiffly up and down. Such excitement sometimes leads to possessions by loa, the drums being important in inducing such possession, as some persons are conditioned to specific rhythms, and that whenever these rhythms are heard possession is induced. Or it may just be a signal, as where there is a battery of drums—which, in most cases there is—signals for the smaller motions come from one drum, and for grosser motions from another.

While there is choreography in the sense that the dancers must meet certain persons at certain places and times in relation to the general movement around the pole, improvisation between is allowed, and no exact concept of a dance "piece" exists. Once the form of the song has "set," the singing tends to follow a regular pattern. The drum rhythms may develop progressively, and in so doing may alter the basic form of the dance. The dance may lead toward any mood: humor, subdued invocation, intensity or speed, and one may sense from the spirit of the gathering what is likely to happen, and though the drummers may restrain or excite the dancers, there is always spontaneity present. The dance may end in three minutes or in thirty; the drummers may be tired, the song leader may be dissatisfied with the participation, or the loa being supplicated may require only brief and nominal recognition.

Form and Function of the Dance in Bali

By Claire Holt & Gregory Bateson

T O AN anthropologist, next to the question of who, when, how, and why certain members of a given society dance, arises the problem of the relationship of the peculiar character of the dance to the character of the people concerned, and to the whole pattern of their culture. What is the relationship between the movements characteristic of a given dance, and the typical gestures and postures in daily life of the very people who perform it? Gesture and posture in daily life are certainly expressive of a people's character, but how are their gestures and postures in a stylized, heightened, and intensified form, as they appear in the dance, related to their particular character?

Why, for instance, is the Balinese dance so totally different from the dance forms of any people in the Western hemisphere? And why, moreover, while having quite a number of affinities in the basic technique with other Indonesian dances, are some of the Balinese dances so strikingly different from the dances of even the Javanese, who are their closest neighbors, only a few miles to the west? The introduction to the dances of Bali given in films in the seminar demonstrated a few of the points raised here.

As a point of departure, the first film showed a Balinese wood-carver at work. He sits cross-legged and relaxed on the ground, and his nimble hands carefully manipulate the chisel, chipping away the yielding wood bit by bit. An Iatmul wood-carver who is seen next tensely hacks away at his wood-carving while crouching. And while obviously the work of the Iatmul does not require the precision and fineness of that of the Balinese, one can state from experience that a Balinese working at an even larger and cruder piece would still proceed with much greater and more meticulous precision than the Iatmul, and with none of the Iatmul's rapid, intense gestures.

Examples along similar lines could be multiplied. People at work in Bali will be observed to use the minimum of effort. They have developed a peculiar separateness of their limbs, and do not engage the body, chest, back, when they have to do things with their hands and arms. Often only the arm, the hand, and the individual fingers will move, without engaging the rest of the body. It was clear in the film of the Iatmul wood-carver that while he worked he was straining to an undue extent the muscles of his whole body.

A feeling of relaxation and detachment characterizes the movements of the Balinese in daily life, whether they are cutting rice or carving a temple wall, preparing a meal, or arranging fruit in the market place. A similar but even more cultivated form of detachment can be detected in some of their ritual dances. So, for instance, the stately processional temple dance, the Redjang, which was shown in films next, demonstrated the slow circular progress of a series of female figures with trailing skirts who at intervals, between a series of stately steps, paused to incline their bodies while slowly swinging their fans. One by one they complete their round in almost spellbound tranquillity in which there is no climax, no variation, but a seemingly endless chain of repetitious movement; then, suddenly, as casually as if she had just finished an errand, a dancer walks off across the court at an ordinary gait, while her companions continue their calm circling.

In contrast to the stately and slow Redjang processional is the Legong dance performed by two small girls aged about eight or nine. With a swiftness and agility that is amazing to any dance expert, Balinese Legong dancers move and flutter over the open dance space, in small rapid, staccato steps, jerking their heads, twisting their arms, and swaying their incredibly nimble little bodies with a precision rivalling that of our robot Rockettes. Their dance can last for an hour or longer. It is supposed to depict a story. But the plot is almost undiscernible, and serves only as an outline to determine the pattern of the choreographic figures and dance gestures which typify Legong dances no matter what part of the legend is being played.

The girls, like our ballet dancers, are puppets par excellence. There is not a trace of individuality in them. The only variation is the degree of perfection to which they have mastered the stylized movements, and a trace of difference due to the fact that of two identical dancers, one is made to perform a "male," and the other a "female" rôle in the story. Legong dances are performed on festive occasions, usually in the temple court, and, like many other dances or dance-plays, are regarded as an offering to the gods.

The next dance shown on the screen was Djoged. A dance girl, also pre-adolescent, is the center of attention. She is a skilful and trained dancer, wears and elaborate and beautiful costume with a special type of dance crown decorated with flowers, and plies the indispensable fan. The style of her dance is similar to that of the Legong, but the movements and pattern are simplified and slower. From the audience male dance partners come out in turn to dance opposite her. Unlike the dance girl they are not specifically trained although some of them are very skilful. With varying degree of accomplishment and grace they posture and circle near the girl dancer, sometimes moving away only to turn back suddenly and approach her again. At no time do the partners touch each other save for an exceptionally daring pat on the arm or shoulder which an extravagant or flirtatious partner will permit himself. This provokes laughter from the audience. To the western observer there is not a trace of emotion visible in the dance girl, and he may wonder how such a completely detached figure could possibly attract the male dancers. Her whole bearing is "noli me tangere." This Djoged is the most popular form of social dancing in Bali, and it is natural therefore that when a Balinese, or, for that matter, any other Indonesian sees our manner of social dancing, with the forthright sexuality and closeness of its contact, he thinks it indecent and crude. On the other hand, our young males are not attracted to, and do not dance with, nine and ten year old girls.

It should be added that sometimes the rôle of the female dancer in the Djoged is filled by a young boy who takes the place of the dance girl, is dressed exactly like her, and is correspondingly feminine and detached in his movements.

A purely male dance is the Baris, representing the exercises of warriors. In recent times stories have been woven into the Baris, and thus a kind of dance-drama evolved in which the stylized movements of the actual dancers closely followed the style of the old war dances. Upon Baris one can hinge a few of the underlying principles of Balinese dance. Imagine a dance in which no jumping, leaping, steady whirling, running, bending of the torso from the waist occurs. Legs and arms form angles in the air; the only emphasis is provided by the hands with spread fingers, and by the sharply turning head.

It seems at intervals as if something forces the dancers into startled jerks. There is no suppleness or continuity in any of the dancer's movements. Quite different from Baris and its stilted style, is the comparatively modern Kebyar, which could best be described as a flirtatious solo dance by a man or boy, the moods of which closely follow the moods of the music. The dance is performed in a seated position. The film showed one of Bali's renowned dance-masters giving a lesson in Kebyar to a young boy. The method of instruction consisted mainly of the teacher leading and pushing the limbs and the body of the pupil into the proper positions until the pupil could get a proper feel of the postures. From time to time the teacher dances before the pupil so that the latter can imitate his movements, but again and again he kneels or crouches close behind the boy and, getting hold of his wrists, forces him to bend and undulate his body—teacher and pupil becoming, as it were, one.

Despite the supple grace and soft sways which occur in the dance, it is always punctuated by a very precise and marked accent of the head or of the hands. Long phrases are brought to a stop with a sharp accent. There was for that reason a curious comparison between the Balinese boy, a novice at dancing, and a skilled professional Hindu dancer who tried to learn Kebyar from the same master, and whose efforts were also shown in the film. For the Hindu dancer the greatest difficulty was to master these very neat, precise accents, sudden jerks and stops, which punctuate the Balinese Kebyar, for his native art, compared with that of Bali, has a much greater continuity of softly flowing movements.

In recent years Kebyar has become one of the favorite dances with which the Balinese entertain foreign tourists. Its gay and flirtatious mood, combined with high technical accomplishment of the dancer, who always stays close to the ground, half-sitting and half-kneeling, and only from time to time changing his place by peculiar hops without actually rising, appeals to foreigners.

A peculiar feature in Balinese life is the widespread phenomenon of trance which in the religious life as well as in the dance has become a regulated occurrence. Bali's famous trance-dancers, the Sanghyang, who are very young girls, become divinities, or possessed by spirits of gods. When in a state of trance they dance in a manner similar to the Legong. There is a regular procedure to put these little girls into presumably auto-hypnotic trance and again to bring them out of it, by means of incense, chants, rhythmical movement, etc.

These ritual preliminaries, however, are quite different in the case of kris dancers—those who bear a dagger called a kris. Usually kris dancers are men or boys who appear in a group as supporters of the Barong (a mythical animal figure associated with "white" or positive, benevolent magic) and as antagonists to the traditional figure of the witch, Rangda. After stepping about in stylized dance manner, with the kris upraised, each dancer in turn attacks the witch. A short fight ensues in which the dancer is very tense and the witch completely relaxed. She only waves her magic cloth. The dancer then falls backwards to the ground in a state of trance. He is aroused from this state by the Barong, and arises in a somnambulistic state of entranced fury, amok against himself. He directs the dagger against his own chest now. Repeatedly, with convulsive movements, he pushes the kris against his own body (oddly enough without actually wounding himself, as a rule) until he falls down in a cramp or in convulsions, writhing on the ground. At a given moment a number of the kris dancers can be seen entranced, jerking their bodies backwards and fitfully pressing the kris against their chest, then falling to the ground. They are then carried away and brought to by means of sprinkling of holy water and other established means.

A variant of the kris-dance, one performed by women in a certain village of South Bali (in response to European suggestions) was shown in the next film. It took place at a great festive occasion in the temple court where all sorts of ritualistic dances were performed. The female kris dancers appeared in a stately procession, showly advancing with upraised kris. After having reached the dance space, the files broke up and each individual dancer began to move about until at a given moment, to the accompaniment of accelerating music, one after the other, as if affected by a rapidly spreading contagion, they began, with a short leap, to swing up their daggers and push them against their chest, bending forward over the dagger-point pressed close to the collar-bone. It was observed that these climax movements of bending forward and downward by the women during the kris-dance were in peculiar contrast to the climactic posture of the men, who jerk backwards when pressing the kris against their chest. Aside from the possible symbolic eroticism of this difference, it is noteworthy that the entranced individuals are able to remember to observe this formality at the height of their paroxysm. Before long the whole dance space becomes a scene of wild ecstasy. All over the place, figures of women with long streaming hair leap and sway, boring their kris, as it were, into their chests, bending over the weapons. In one corner a male kris-dancer writhes in convulsions on the ground while the priest, sprinkling holy water out of a beaker, moves between the dancers. Villagers carry off twisting bodies of other dancers who have reached a dangerous state of entranced ecstasy, and wrest the daggers from their cramped fists.

This brief description of a few of the Balinese dances cannot, of course, evoke a clear vision of the dancers' appearance and of their movements in space and time. However, one can state that among the typical features characterizing Balinese dances, the following can be observed:

1: Complete lack of visible emotional expression. Even in dance-drama, where emotions are enacted, they are conveyed through a traditional pattern of stylized gestures which, effective as they may be, leave no room for interpretation by the personal expression of the individual dancer. In short, complete detachment reigns throughout, whether it be a ritual, a social dance, a drama or a pure dance-spectacle. The only very important exceptions are the grotesque and comic characters. In delightful burlesques they indulge during their rough-house scenes, in violent emotional reactions which, however, are often either startled surprise or fear. Supplanting emotion is a tenseness of a strange detached kind, which in our terminology can be likened to a state of trance, or possession, as the Indonesian would term it.

2: All dances, whether male or female, with the exception of ancient ritual processionals, are characterized by intermittent sharp accents. These can be a sequence of precise, sharp, staccato steps, little taps occuring at intervals, or sudden jerks of the dancer's head which punctuate a dance phrase, or a sudden stop and pulling up of the whole figure as though the dancer were suddenly startled.

3: The fundamental posture in female secular dances involves a markedly outcurved spine with the buttocks pushed out. The torso of the male dancer is comparatively rigid. The pubic area is never pushed forward, nor do undulating movements prevalent in Indian and Polynesian dances occur. In both male and female dances the limbs form angles, and there is a tendency to pull up the shoulders with upraised and out-turned angular elbows pointed upwards so that the head sinks between them and the neck disappears.

4: The technique of Balinese dancing calls for extraordinary control of the limbs, for endurance, and in many cases for meticulous precision.

5: The Balinese, like all Indonesian dancers, never tend away from the ground. They do not dance upward and away from the earth, but move on it, along its surface, in slow circles or lines, rapid semi-circles and serpentines, and in a sudden zig-zag of short duration. In some cases they dance seated on the ground. Elevation above the ground occurs, as an exception, only when the Sanghyang, the little girl trance dancers, mount upon the shoulders of the men who then carry them, unsupported, through the dance space. Standing on the shoulders of their carriers the Sanghyang continue dancing with their bodies, arms, and heads, high above the ground.

6: In Balinese choreography, sudden changes of direction are a marked feature. With a sharp accent, semi-circles or lines are reversed. Intermittently the dancer checks her swift progress with a jerk, and proceeds in the opposite direction. Again the old processional dances are an exception.

Perhaps an attempt could now be made to relate some of the peculiarities of the Balinese dance to the Balinese character and temperament, inasmuch as these have been a subject of anthropological study. To a foreign observer the striking feature of the Balinese scene is the seemingly subdued and even tone of social relations among the Balinese. There is an outward equanimity bordering on indifference. Even friendly gaiety or sullenness do not carry any feeling of pulsating emotions of the order we know. Rarely does one discover any passions given expression at village gatherings or courts, at cremation ceremonies, temple feasts or in the market place. It has been stated that owing to an observed pattern of frustration which the Balinese undergoes in early childhood, his emotions or emotional expressions are suppressed or even paralyzed; as is, to a lesser degree, similarly achieved in England. The detachment which characterizes Balinese dancing would thus not be a departure from normal life, but an extension and intensification to further cold passion of everyday Balinese behavior.

Institutionalized trance, which finds an outlet in the dance, can be traced to the strong auto-suggestive forces at work in every animistic society, where possession by spirits and deities in a formalized manner plays such an important ritualistic rôle. It is suggested that certain Balinese trance-dances, especially the kris dances, are relevant to the Balinese character structure. Frustrated impulses of a violent nature which in childhood were compensated by tantrums, find sublimated parallels—in an adult society where imitative pressure requires an outward equanimity—in the self-directed violence of the kris dance. This is, however, not even symbolically a total expression of the suppressed stresses, for the witch in the kris dance (possibly a mother symbol representing the social environment) is not touched or harmed by the dancers' attacks; she only waves, and through her magic the dancers must turn the weapons against themselves until in frenzied convulsions they roll on the ground—in itself no doubt some release from inhibited tensions, whether the trance is autosuggestive and intense, or merely a dance-pattern.

Like most Indonesians, the Balinese dislike wide open spaces. They will never build a house without hemming it in with trees and walls. Fear of spirits pervades life and all activities. The "happy islanders" are really a fear-haunted people, and endless precautions are always taken to prevent or counteract the ever-lurking but undefined dangers. One must be on guard always. Perhaps these fears are reflected in Balinese dance as well as in its repressed life. One could venture the suggestion that leaving the ground is dangerous, and one must bend toward it and move along it; and only such chosen and semi-divine beings as the Sanghyang in trance may soar for a moment, and stay above the ground for any length of time.

Angularity, precision, and clean-cut details are characteristic not only of the dance, but also of traditional Balinese pictorial and plastic art. It may be pointed out here that spirits always travel in straight lines. They are misled by change of direction. One confuses them by turning cremation towers in the middle of a procession, and does not build a house in a straight line with the entrance gate.

In the course of their history the people of Bali learned many things from other people, among them the Hindu-Javanese and the Chinese. Many features of Balinese art, including the dance, bear unmistakable traces of these influences, yet none of them were completely decisive in the moulding of Balinese art forms. The peculiarities of Balinese character were a factor in the selection and adaptation of foreign elements, and in the final shaping of their creations whether of stone, cloth, or motion; painted, chiselled, or danced.

In searching for this cultural temperament, this mass character, the anthropologist can find in the study of the dance corroborative material for his observations, as well as clues which will direct his research toward new aspects. One field which still awaits exploration is the question of how far a dominant kinesthetic awareness of certain parts of the body is related to psychological factors. If posture and movement of an individual are closely interdependent with his psychological state, would not stylized posture and gesture in the dance of a people be relevant to a general psychological trend in their life?

Other questions, too, still await an answer from future study and research. For instance: Are peoples who have belly-dances, with rhythmic, rotating movements of the pelvic region different in cultural temperament from those whose torsos and hips are rigid in dancing? If so, wherein does the difference lie, and is the mass character of the people to be considered similar to that of their dance and expressed by it, or opposite to it and compensated by it? As for instance in the case of the above-mentioned belly-dance versus the rigid pelvis. Or, for another instance, are peoples whose dances call for high leaps and jumps more aggressive, braver, or more cruel than peoples who only step or shuffle along the ground, or are they less so? Does a predilection for soft, continuous, undulating movements disclose a particular psychological feature or total character different from that of peoples whose movements in the dance are abrupt? What is this difference?

31 - 161